I never had the oppor Lee-Knight. But thanks to this book by Ruth Lee-Knight, I now have a glimpse of Lorie and the talents and passions of this remarkable person. Her vibrancy comes through to me in her words to her parents, "Just wait 'til you see the house I'm going to build you!" So much confidence and vision and unselfishness. Another picture of Lorie that struck me was her habit of going for runs at Olympic Stadium in Athens, with a view of the Acropolis—such a blending of youthful energy and timelessness. During her study abroad experience, Lorie was truly having *the time of her life*. The second half of the book is the story of parents wrestling with the senseless loss of a beloved daughter and their discovery of the meaning of God's promise to Israel, and to them: "how I carried you on eagles' wings and brought you to myself" (Exodus 19:3 - 4). Lorie's creative medium was art and drawing, transforming canvasses into beautiful works of art. Ruth's medium is words, and we are privileged to share in her pain and struggle as she puts them on paper. Ruth finds comfort in knowing that Lorie is now at peace and, if she could, would say to her parents: "Remember, I am always with you, but will be waiting with big hugs when it is time for each of you to join me. God **is** in charge." Ruth replies, "I will search for you in the flowers of my mind where trees sway and where you wait until my own sun sets." Thank you, Ruth, for sharing your story with us.

—Doug Shantz, Ph. D.
Professor of Christian Thought
Endowed Chair
Department of Religious Studies

For Gwen ~
~ With Love

THE MOUNTIE'S GIRL

RUTH LEE-KNIGHT

THE MOUNTIE'S GIRL
Copyright © 2013 by Ruth Lee-Knight. All rights reserved.

Unless otherwise indicated, all Scripture quotations are taken from The Message. Copyright © 1993, 1994, 1995, 1996, 2000, 2001, 2002. Used by permission of NavPress Publishing Group. • Scripture quotations marked (ESV) are from The Holy Bible, English Standard Version® (ESV®), copyright © 2001 by Crossway, a publishing ministry of Good News Publishers. Used by permission. All rights reserved.

ISBN: 978-1-77069-892-5

Word Alive Press
131 Cordite Road, Winnipeg, MB R3W 1S1
www.wordalivepress.ca

Cataloguing in Publication information may be obtained through Library and Archives Canada

ACKNOWLEDGEMENTS

Reverend Ivor Ottrey for his enduring love and support and for his dedication to intercessions on behalf of Jack and me. He has provided the book with a heartfelt Foreword.

Reverend Canon Howard Green for being a stalwart friend, for sharing his unique insight and for writing a special recommendation for this book.

Doug Shantz for his encouragement and suggestions for the incomplete manuscript and for writing a notable recommendation for my book.

Susan Himann for her compassion and encouragement upon reading the manuscript's first draft.

Jack Lee-Knight, my supportive mate, who believed in my strong compunction to share our lovely daughter and her story with the public.

Word Alive Press who compassionately guided me through the publication process.

CONTENTS

FOREWORD

Rev. Canon Ivor Ottrey, B.A., Lth.

I am honored to have been asked to write the foreword for the author, Ruth Lee-Knight. *The Mountie's Girl* tells of the parents' intense love for their treasured and beautiful daughter, Lorie Gaye. It also tells of the terrible and tragic, brutal murder of this very lovely young woman.

It is the moving story beautifully told by a grieving mother twenty-six years after the sad and unforgettable incident. The only real comfort in death, especially a tragic one, is the glorious hope of the resurrection to eternal life through faith in our Lord Jesus Christ, which certain hope, I know Lorie and her dear parents share.

As you read, you will come to know Lorie in all her exuberance and love of life. She was energetic and adventuresome, eager to travel and to learn. She was an accomplished artist and was studying architecture, in which she was excelling. To be with Lorie was to be alive with her joy and laughter; she was a young woman with a truly magnetic personality.

In addition to all her parents reveal about Lorie, I am sure that as you read letters of condolences from friends, fellow students, professors, and other acquaintances you will realize what an exceptional person Lorie was and how much she was loved by so many, for she was not only beautiful physically, but beautiful as a person who exuded love and in turn was loved deeply by others.

I remember Lorie with joy and gladness. Indeed, one could not help but to love and admire the whole family, who were a great blessing to the community.

I heartily commend *The Mountie's Girl* to you, as it is beautifully written and illustrated with photos and copies of some of Lorie's art. You will want to read this book, which tells of a precious daughter who touched so many lives wherever she went.

In loving memory of our golden daughter,
Lorie Gaye Lee-Knight, who was only loaned to us.

Jack and I were married in 1958 at St. Andrew's Anglican Church in my hometown of Humboldt, Saskatchewan, a bustling town that served a large agricultural district. Following nursing classes at Regina College and nurses training at Regina General Hospital, I had returned to work at St. Elizabeth's Hospital in Humboldt. Jack and I met soon after the RCMP had transferred him there. He had chosen to work in the field of detachments and so, following our marriage, began years of postings at various points in Saskatchewan. Our son, Christopher Todd, was born in 1959 at Humboldt and our daughter, Lorie Gaye, was born two and a half years later in Spalding, Saskatchewan, during our posting at nearby Naicam. Our family was to be transferred to six more communities before Jack retired.

If we had not been posted at Onion Lake, I would likely not have learned of its historical significance. With Fort Pitt to the east and Frog Lake to the west we were situated in the midst of dramas that had occurred in the 1800's. There had been battles between policemen and natives, killings and pillaging. I was profoundly moved as I walked through the Frog Lake cemetery, the final resting place for several victims of the Frog Lake Massacre of 1885.

Goodsoil, located in the boreal forest of Northwest Saskatchewan, introduced us not only to its unique spruce-scented air but to the beauty of Lac des Isles and to the Waterhen and Beaver Rivers. Square dancing in the community centre introduced us to many locals. We have returned many times to renew acquaintances and to visit old haunts.

Moosomin provided us with a church to attend and a Sunday School for our children. We made life-long friends and had access to more amenities. Kamsack is where we also made good friends. Nearby Madge Lake gave opportunities for camping, swimming and boating. Our children learned to ski on a wintry hill. We may never have experienced that lake had we not been moved to Kamsack.

At Prince Albert, we had the excitement of buying our first house. There were many amenities, and Little Red River Park became our favorite recreation site. Lorie had an exceptional teacher who greatly encouraged Lorie's artistic abilities. Three years was the longest time we stayed in any location until we moved to Swift Current. We remained there for almost thirteen years before we retired.

But there was a life-changing tragedy awaiting us, and that is the subject of this book.

Twenty-six years after Lorie Gaye's death I have, at last, found the strength to chronicle her life of only twenty-four years. She died a cruel and tragic death, but her spirit lives on in the many hearts she touched. Her prolific works of art are ever present reminders for her parents, other family members, and friends.

Like an exotic bird she sailed into and out of people's lives, always needing to fly off to experience other people and other places, absorbing beauty and leaving love wherever she went. She was in love with life and seemed to be in a hurry to absorb all things joyous and beautiful wherever she encountered them.

This book, written with a mother's love, describes all ages and stages of our beautiful daughter. This way, no matter at what stage or phase people encountered her, they can be introduced to all that came before and after—the whole person. Readers will understand what a special person her parents have lost and miss terribly.

The second purpose of this book is to direct all my revenue from its sales to a special building project. Lorie's poignant exclamation to us, "Just *wait* 'til you see the house I'm going to build *you*," should not be allowed to expire with her last breath, but should be brought to life in a worthy form. It is my intention that all funds that are directed to me will go toward St. Martin's Anglican Church (Calgary) Building Fund.

I never knew what form that promised house would take, but the answer came to me as I walked alone along a nature trail near our cottage on a sunny and windy afternoon. It was August of 2011, and the anniversary of Lorie's death, when I was pondering anew how I could have her life count for something—something more than it already had to her family and friends. There, on that trail, a new and sudden thought was revealed to me, as it seemed I was aligned in perfect harmony with God's will. With wild bluebells and mauve fall asters nodding at my feet, and wind-buffeted treetops all about me, this sudden discernment, clear and complete, seemed to waft gently down upon my being. *What a gift! Perfect!* I thought. The house Lorie spoke of with such feeling would be a house of God that her dad and I had long awaited and desired. It seemed Lorie spoke one word with gusto: "Yes!"

The third purpose of this book is detailed in the postscript.

PART ONE

THE MOUNTIE'S GIRL

Lorie Gaye was the only baby in the nursery of the Spalding, Saskatchewan hospital that cold winter morning. It was February 15, 1962, and she had missed being born on Valentine's Day by one hour and forty-five minutes. Pink and bald with rosebud lips, Lorie Gaye weighed in at seven pounds, eleven ounces. She was lovely and healthy. We named her after a vibrant and joyful friend and our Lorie lived up to those attributes. As it happened, Lorie's younger cousin was named after her. "So, who had the baby last night?" I heard the inquiry from the first staff member coming in for the 7-3 shift.

"Oh, that's the Mountie's girl," the night nurse's aide replied. "She's the Valentine gift her parents had wanted. They already have a two-year-old boy, so everybody's happy. And the Mountie sat at the doctor's side to witness the birth. He's braver than a lot of dads."

****

Lorie Gaye was only two weeks old when the phone call came. At the time I was comfortably settled on the sofa with our son, Christopher Todd, happily playing at my feet. The baby, fast asleep, was a warm presence bundled in my arms. Jack was working in his office just on the other side of the hall door adjoining our new detachment living quarters. His new pup, Kip, an intelligent German shepherd, was his constant companion. We were a happy family. Snow was piled high on either side of the walk to our front door and the office door beside it, and for a short time we were impervious to the world outside our family circle. The office phone rang, and I heard Jack in conversation. Then there was silence for several minutes. Christopher and I looked up when the office door opened, and Jack walked into the residence. Kip followed his master. At my first glance I knew Jack was in his serious mode. I tightened my hold on Baby Lorie.

"Just got a call from the member at Onion Lake. He wants to know what colors we want the bedrooms painted," Jack paused as I look blankly back at him. I noticed he looked a little shocked. A small tingling of fear crept into my neck muscles. I was afraid to ask, but could not help myself.

"What do you *mean*? What does *he* mean?" I managed.

"Seems we're being transferred there. He thought I might have heard from Sub-Division. He says I'm supposed to take over Onion Lake the first week of April."

"What's an Onion Lake? Where is it?" My voice quivered.

"I don't really know. Somewhere up north, I guess."

Upon examining a map we discovered the community was located near the Saskatchewan/Alberta border north of both Lloydminster and the North Saskatchewan River. I knew Jack was disappointed. He had worked so hard to put the Naicam detachment office in order and make it run efficiently. He had set up every aspect of the office after our move from an old, makeshift building. We both knew that transfers were a part of our lives with Jack being in detachment work. We just thought the Force would have been a bit more thoughtful than to move a member and his wife when she had just given birth. And, the fact that this transfer was only a 'sideways' move, not one involving a promotion, was a bitter pill to swallow. Then, of course, Sub-Division had not given Jack the courtesy of a heads up regarding a transfer in the near future.

Lorie was never to know her first home in the pleasant community east of Saskatoon, Saskatchewan. Nor would she know the good friends we had made in Naicam. I was never able to show her off as I had her brother where he was born in my hometown of Humboldt located an hour east of Saskatoon. Our daughter's start in life seemed to signal many negative occurrences that surrounded her life.

Onion Lake was a disappointment from the moment we first heard its name. Jack was to work long, difficult hours there, usually alone. While he functioned on short, infrequent sleep and spent most of the time working away from the detachment office, I was alone and unhappy. I was concerned about our young son having no playmates, and I missed not having other women to visit with. I needed to share our clever, handsome son and beautiful baby with others but rarely had that opportunity.

Among the many disappointments and concerns that we experienced upon our arrival at Onion Lake was the discovery of a mice infestation. Jack discovered a window had been left open when workmen were building a bomb shelter in the basement. This gave easy access to mice seeking a nice dry place to live. The doors were left open while the movers carried in our furniture and several packing boxes. We were all tired, stiff and out of sorts. This mouse discovery seemed more than I could bear. Jack knew how upset I was and he promised to buy traps and cheese the next day. He also said he would find a cat. While I searched for the cartons holding our bedding and tin goods, Jack set up the crib and checked out his office. Once I had beds made for everyone I heated the baby's bottle and our soup on the gas stove. Kip eagerly gulped the food I had set out for him. When the movers were finished we were able to close the doors and heat the house up. That chilly April evening there were no neighbors to be seen in any direction, only lonely, desolate looking landscape. As I looked out the windows at the bleak and lonely surroundings, I felt a shiver of fear run through me, wondering about our future in this unwelcoming place.

Meanwhile, Baby Lorie developed some suspicious looking eruptions on the top of her fuzzy blond scalp. With the vigilance of a protective mother, I had terrible visions of mice bedding down on her warm little head during the dark of night and leaving her with an infection. I gave Jack the alarm and insisted we make the drive to Lloydminster to have the baby seen by a physician. The trip across the North Saskatchewan River via a precarious looking ferry did nothing to calm my shattered nerves. The physician could not tell what had caused the infection, but he felt the mice were likely suspects. So he prescribed an antibiotic ointment for the baby's scalp eruptions, and they cleared up in due time. Her strawberry blond hair grew in curly, becoming the envy of her friends. Only her mother knew the awful nightmare vision of mice being attracted to her beautiful warm head.

I had wanted to have Lorie baptized, and even that event was difficult to arrange. The Anglican minister at Lloydminster did not know us, so he wanted us to attend Sunday morning services before making arrangements. I knew this would not be possible, since weekends were Jack's busiest times, and I knew he could not be away from responsibilities in his detachment area. The minister reluctantly agreed to a private service mid-week. We were a small, lonely little family that day, with no one present to support us as we welcomed Lorie Gaye into the Church. We had been able to have Christopher Todd baptized at St. Andrew's in Humboldt with my parents and friends in attendance. There were photos in our family album of smiling faces sharing the event.

There was no one to take photos of Lorie's special day, nor see her in another of her lovely, dainty dresses, her blond hair making a soft halo about her well-shaped head. In any case, we had to hurry back to Onion Lake, as Jack could never relax when away from his detachment. He invited the storeowner and his wife to come to the house for a celebratory drink to mark the occasion. They spent a pleasant hour with us but could not be away from their business for long, so it seemed as if Lorie's special day held little significance. That bothered me a lot, and I felt as if my little family and I were more prisoners than those individuals who were actually behind Onion Lake detachment bars for a few hours now and then. Once alone with the children I took a few photos, so there would be something to validate Lorie's special day. But I was left with an empty feeling.

My children had to have been negatively affected by my unhappy state. When Jack joined his family for an hour here or a few minutes there it was cause for celebration, always followed by disappointment. I loved watching him wrestling on the floor or giving them horsey rides on his large, highly polished knee-high uniform boots. Too soon, he was called away to the phone, the door, or to the two-way radio. His meals were too often short-notice sandwiches, which I would hand to him as he started up the police car. Another problem had him rushing away, his hot meal untouched, his wife and children sad.

I knew the children saw me crying on occasion. I suffered sleep deprivation, as I could never relax when Jack was alone and away working at night or when I knew he was in a situation that could be dangerous for him. When he came home late, it was often with prisoners and the Justice of the Peace. The office was just below the master bedroom, so that loud, often inebriated voices, heavy boots, clanging cell doors, clacking typewriter, phone, and radio did nothing to lull me to sleep. I know I was, at times, short with the children when they were, just as much as me, the innocent victims of our living conditions. It was with great relief when, after one year and three months, we were transferred out. Jack was about to be promoted to Corporal.

****

Goodsoil became home. The village was located in an attractive park setting in northwest Saskatchewan and was bordered by the Beaver River to the south with the Waterhen River and the Meadow Lake Provincial Park to the north. Lorie, now sixteen months and Chris, almost four, were able to run free on the large, grassy and fenced property. Kip, our German shepherd, and Blackie, the cat, also enjoyed all this new space. Other children were attracted to our yard, with its swing set and large sand box, so Lorie and Chris soon had playmates to share their happy days. During rainy times or on cold winter days the children played in our basement. The bomb shelter seemed like a fun place in which to play house. Lorie had an array of dolls down there, and Chris had a collection of boy toys. This shelter was one of hundreds the federal government had had built during the Cold War.

In the open space of the basement Chris also practised stick handling and shooting the puck with his trusty hockey stick. I often found Lorie drawing pictures with pencils or crayons on scrap paper I kept the children supplied with. Even at her tender age she was amazingly adept at replicating people and things within her experience. I often kept a drawing I came upon to show her dad at the first opportunity. We were both impressed, but little did we realize we had spawned a talented artist.

Lorie was also attracted to water, eventually trying everything aquatic. Her first lake experience occurred at Lac des Isles close to Goodsoil. At sixteen months while paddling in the shallow water she decided to copy her brother's attempts at swimming. As I helped Chris I turned to find her floating face down. I called for Chris to go back to shore while I lunged toward Lorie and grabbed onto her sun suit. I can still see the water rivulets running down her sunbathed face, her look of surprised pleasure. I was gripped with terror thinking how badly this scenario could have turned out. I felt guilty for having taken this risk with both children in the water where no possible quick help would have been available to us. That day brought back memories of some months earlier. Following her bath I had dressed her in white tights and new white leather boots. After turning my back for a few moments, I discovered she had crawled back into the little blue plastic tub of water, and was sitting, leather boots and all, happily playing with her bath toys.

****

Our daughter was always adventurous, and this sometimes got her into difficulties. One day at Goodsoil she put her brother's favorite stuffed toy, Yogi the Bear, into their little red wagon and "went for a walk." When I discovered she was missing from the yard, Chris and I went looking for her. She was quickly found in the deep, weedy ditch just beyond our yard. She still had the red wagon but there was no sign of Yogi. Chris was very upset so we kept searching until we finally had to give up. The toy must have bounced out at some point, but Lorie had not realized she was pulling an empty wagon. Her big brother was very upset at the loss of his bedtime companion, and for years he reminded her of the incident.

One wet spring day, our children were out playing, attired appropriately in jackets, hats and rubber boots. Like any children they were attracted to little puddles of water and were happily playing near the house. Suddenly a concerned looking Chris came in to tell me that his sister was stuck. He had always taken a position of looking out for his young sister. I hurried to the scene just on the other side of our fence to where Lorie stood in the muddy garden. This looked to me like a two-person rescue was required, so I calmed Lorie, who was by now upset that her feet would not move for her, telling her I would bring her dad to help. Luckily, Jack was in the office across the driveway from our living quarters. When I hastily explained the dilemma, he went directly to the scene. Lorie was very relieved to have her daddy lift her up out of that trouble. The Mountie's girl was safe and sound in his protective arms. Her little white boots remained stubbornly in the mud. By then, I had donned my own boots and with some careful maneuvering was able to pull her boots up and through the fence.

****

That fall, Jack and a friend drove into our yard with a newly killed black bear in the back of the friend's truck. Jack was thrilled to have shot the bear that was a more rare cinnamon colour. Chris and I ran out to admire it, as did the second man who was stationed with us at the time. The guard, who had been hired to watch over a prisoner in the jail cell, also came out for a moment. Kip, all bristling, took a special interest in this creature with the strange scent. He was in his protective mode, sniffing and growling in turn. With all the excitement going on, Lorie, who had been positioned on the potty chair in the bathroom, decided to go outside to see for herself. I had just run out with the camera to get a few shots of the hunters with the hunted when Lorie appeared, barefoot and bare bottomed. She looked darling wearing only a little white sweater, with blond curls around her rosy face. I quickly took a photo of her. The young policeman appeared very uncomfortable to see this scantily clothed child, so I hastily returned her to the house to find the rest of her clothes. In subsequent years, her family would remind her that there had been a lot of bear/bare that day.

****

The following summer, still at our Goodsoil posting, the children were out playing with their friends. Climbing trees was apparently on their agenda that sunny day. When I heard sounds of distress coming through the kitchen window I hurried out. Chris and the others were all looking upward at a large poplar tree just outside the kitchen. Who could it be, but Lorie Gaye who was stranded on a high branch? She had climbed beyond my reach, and she seemed unable to move. Once again, we were all fortunate that Jack was working in his office. The alarm went out, and within moments the Mountie's girl was being rescued by her daddy. She was a little shaken but in a few minutes was again playing happily. Our little girl learned early that taking risks was okay as someone, usually her dad, would be there to help whenever needed. If only that could have been true when she grew up and moved away.

****

We experienced both excitement and sadness when we learned of our transfer from Goodsoil. We would miss the beauty of the forested area and especially of Lac des Isles. Our family had spent many happy hours at the beach and, on occasion, in the RCMP boat after Jack had completed checks on boaters. In subsequent summers we would return to that lake where we camped on its shores and where both Chris and Lorie learned to water ski. At the time of our transfer to Moosomin we looked forward to its business district, streetlights, sidewalks, and a church for us to attend with a Sunday school for the children.

The town was located on the number One Highway north east of Yorkton, Saskatchewan near the Manitoba border. I was disappointed that we would have to live in quarters over the post office until the new detachment was built. Another disappointment came when we decided it was kinder to give Kip to a good family in the country rather than confine him in a downtown apartment. Blackie, the cat, would go with us, and we promised the children another dog as soon as we moved into the new quarters. Little did we know that wait would take two years. I assured the children that they would soon have new little friends. Their dad was to be promoted to sergeant. The children easily picked up on our good mood. They played more happily, and I often heard them giggling together. Lorie knew that she would start school in the new town. She seemed excited about the prospects of going to school with her brother.

The downtown apartment over the post office was not a place for active, growing children. They had no yard to play in, but luckily our family made friends with another only a block away. Their children and ours had many a happy hour in the Wilson yard. Elsie and Cliff became our life-long friends. Elsie was a Sunday school teacher at St. Alban's Anglican Church, so our children felt comfortable with her as they became acquainted with their new surroundings. I have pleasant memories of walking to church with the children. I can still see Lorie in her new pretty pink dress, the coat I had made to match, white socks and patent leather shoes. She was a picture with her blond curls.

While Chris and the Wilson children were in school Lorie often had no one to play with. I ached for my little girl having to spend so many hours each day without a playmate. Her toys did not have much appeal if she had to play alone. She filled some of the time drawing and coloring endless pictures. With only one television channel available we made certain to watch the few children's shows. Fortunately, Blackie had produced a batch of darling kittens so for a few weeks Lorie was happy watching over them. One day when she was especially bored I produced a wicker basket and suggested she put the kittens in it for a while. When she became bored again, I suggested she take the basket of kittens over to show Mrs. Wilson, so off she went down the street. Elsie much admired them and cuddled each one for a few minutes before she had to get back to her own housework. Lorie returned home, a little happier than when she'd left. It lifted my spirits as well as Lorie's at least for a short time. I have always blessed my dear friend for taking a few minutes out of her busy day to give Lorie a little joy. She knew about our difficult living conditions. Lorie never forgot that kindness, and Elsie became one of the favourite people in her life, as well as in mine.

Lorie's first day in school was traumatic for both her and her mother. Even though I had built up a positive picture of this upcoming experience for Lorie, she did not warm to the idea. Apparently the upheaval of moving had been difficult enough to change Lorie's mind about this school idea. It did not seem to help that Chris had enjoyed Grade One in Goodsoil, and his first years of school at MacLeod School in Moosomin. Dressed in new clothes, Lorie walked with Chris and me to her first day. Once we met her teacher we were invited into the classroom. Lorie sat at her assigned desk, but seemed overcome by the room full of children she did not know. She would not let me out of her sight, so I sat at the small desk beside her, and we listened to the teacher's welcoming remarks. She started to read a story. I thought that was an appropriate time to leave, but at each attempt I made, Lorie grabbed onto me. Her face was red and she was perspiring profusely, a look of terror in her eyes. I kept reminding her that none of the other children had mothers with them. Soon it was clear that the teacher wanted me to leave, and I felt there was no other choice. As I approached the door, Lorie followed me, clutching my clothing and crying loudly.

I can never forget the fear in my little girl's eyes. I felt torn between wanting to hold her and believing I may not be helping her by prolonging the inevitable. Walking away from that school door was one of the hardest things I ever had to do as a mother. My stomach muscles churned at the distress. I could not relax until I returned an hour later to wait for Lorie to appear. I walked both children to school for a few days until Lorie felt comfortable going with just her brother. Soon she was joined by a girl whom we discovered lived nearby. The girls became friends and then made it a habit of walking together. Chris was relieved he no longer had to accompany his sister to school. At that point he was more interested in making friends with other boys. Peace settled on our household. Still, I wished I had been able to take my little girl's fear away, but like many situations in years to follow, I could not always stand between her and the problems she had to face.

****

Since Moosomin was not far from Regina we could more often visit my parents and sister, Marjorie, and her family there. After two years of enduring the inconvenience of the upstairs quarters next to the RCMP office and over the busy post office, we finally moved into the new quarters with a connecting door to the new RCMP office complex. We were on a residential street, and a new lawn and some trees had been planted in our spacious yard. It was time to keep our promise to the children, so we welcomed Toby, a spunky brown terrier-mix pup, into our family. The children were thrilled, and even Blackie, the cat, tolerated him.

It became routine on Saturdays for the children to get up on their own to play with their pets and to watch television cartoons. It was a time for brother and sister to bond together, also to conspire about who would wake up first to turn on the television. They were learning something about independence and responsibly caring for their pets. One Saturday morning while Jack and I were enjoying a rare sleep-in, Lorie was up before Chris. When I got up I found a note on the kitchen table. Written in Lorie's six-year-old, heavy print was the message, "Daer Mom. I am fou a. I am uot sid with Toby for a walk. Love, Lorie." I could tell that Lorie had persisted in her attempt at printing until she was satisfied that she had conveyed her meaning. Her heavy hand showed her great concentration on the task. I was amused when I found the note, but at Lorie's return I thanked her for her thoughtfulness at writing it. These characteristics of concentration and determination remained with our daughter all of her life. These traits showed in everything she attempted.

That little scrap of paper is still one of my special mementoes from Lorie's childhood. When I read it, I always smile and yet it brings tears to my eyes. My soul reaches back tenderly to a time of innocence when I had both my children safely with me. I can still picture my little daughter wanting to leave a note so that I would not be concerned at her absence; can see her determinedly working on that note. I recall how that trait became stronger with age; she always worked doggedly on school assignments, especially art projects until she was satisfied with the outcome. At university this habit would see her work through the night if she felt it necessary to achieve perfection as she saw it. It is just a little scrap of paper yet it evokes a plethora of heartfelt emotions.

****

Our one year of happy times in the new house and office complex ended when we were moved to Kamsack. This community was northeast of Yorkton, Saskatchewan and near the Manitoba border. Once more, Jack was transferred on a sideways move since Kamsack was a Sergeant's point just as was Moosomin's. It was difficult for us to leave Moosomin and the friends we had made there, but, as usual, I put on a brave face for the children, filling them with positive comments. They would meet a lot of new friends and see things and places they had never seen before. There was a very nice lake and beach near Kamsack, so we would all enjoy that.

Of course, this time Toby would go with us. It was important, especially for our children, that Toby would be moving with us. I knew how traumatic it had been for the children when we had to part with our Kip. He had been like a member of our family. It was also difficult for them to understand how Blackie could just disappear as she had. Their concerns were eased when Fancy, the new kitten eventually joined our family. By then our aging Blackie had disappeared on one of her many all-night wanderings, never to be seen or heard of again. We were used to Blackie's absence on some nights, but she was usually meowing at the door in the morning. When a couple of days past without seeing her I was getting concerned. The children had begun to ask about her. I put them off by saying that she would likely surprise us and turn up as usual. Eventually it became apparent that we had seen the last of Blackie. I knew the children were concerned, but there seemed little I could say to help. We agreed that she must have died of old age. I told them that once we were settled in Kamsack we would get them a new kitten. They seemed satisfied with that prospect, but whenever they saw a photo of Blackie and Kip at play the children grew quiet. I knew they were thinking that now they had lost both those beloved pets. These were the first experiences our children had of losing somethings they had loved. I noticed in new drawings Lorie would sometimes include a large black dog and a black cat. I felt it was her way of honoring these pets and perhaps keeping them for a while longer.

We parked our trailer on a site near the beach at Madge Lake for the two summers we lived in Kamsack. The children and I spent much of the summer there, and Jack usually came for the evening meal. Chris and Lorie were enrolled in swimming lessons that they enjoyed. They had ample time to practise what they had learned. I often joined them when we cavorted in the water. It was refreshingly cool with a sandy bottom. Both children would demonstrate what they had learned in the most recent lesson. When their dad was able to take time for a swim it was always fun for the whole family. Toby would join us for a game of chase the stick. The children learned to climb up on their dad's back and then with much shrieking and laughing they would jump into the water. Later, while I made supper, Lorie and Chris would help their dad make a fire. After eating outdoors we would sit around the fire to catch up on each other's news. The children would sometimes report that they had seen a bear at the wood's edge, or tell about the number of deer they had seen that day. Those were happy times.

One sunny morning when another mother and I were chatting I had looked away from the water for a few moments. When I turned back I saw Lorie trying to make her way toward the beach. I could tell that she was crying. I quickly plunged into the water and as I reached her I said, "What happened, Dear?" I saw that she was favoring one arm.

"When I was diving I slipped and fell on the dock," she sobbed. "My teacher told me to try again, but it hurt too much and I couldn't," she wailed.

"Oh, that's too bad, Honey," I said soothingly. "Let's get to shore and I'll check you out." Back on the beach I found it was her right shoulder that was causing the pain. Her fingers were already a little puffy but their color was good. I gathered her up and took both children along with Toby into Kamsack. "What will the doctor do?" asked a worried Lorie, still sniffing.

"Well, he'll look at your shoulder and have an x-ray taken. Don't worry, it's going to be okay."

At the hospital Lorie and I went to the Emergency Department. Chris stayed in the car reading a comic book and Toby kept him company. The kindly doctor examined

Lorie and then had an x-ray taken. He put a sling on her arm telling her, "Well, my dear, you have a break in your collar bone. You'll have to wear this sling for a few weeks. Try to keep the arm as still as possible so you'll heal well. No more swimming this summer, but next year you'll catch up just fine." The doctor told me the collar bone was in good alignment so it would heal well if the position was maintained. I could see the concern in Lorie's eyes–no swimming, keep still–the news seemed to overwhelm her. I felt tears gathering in my own eyes, but I had to be brave for my little girl.

"Now you can learn to draw with your left hand, " I offered cheerily, We'll pick up some nice books at the library, too. Then let's get back to the lake and stop in for cones at the Snack Shack there," was all I could offer at the moment. Jack brought a television out from town and he set it up under a shady tree beside the trailer.

"Now you'll be able to see all the kid's shows and still watch what's happening on the beach," he offered as he tousled Lorie's hair. I could tell that her dad ached for her as I did. He talked with the swimming instructor who was apologetic about not being more helpful at the time of Lorie's accident. Jack also checked out the dock. When he found much of it covered in a green slime caused by gull deposits, he had the dock scraped. That way he hoped to save any other child from a nasty accident. As Lorie tried drawing with her left hand I noticed she would look up wistfully at children playing in the water. I would sometimes see a look of determination in her face. Perhaps she was thinking that she would one day be a swimming instructor and that she would make sure little children were kept safe. By summer's end Lorie was healed, and she resumed normal activities. She took swim lessons the following summer, and in later years went on to instruct swimming and did life guarding duties. Her young students loved her as she was so helpful and caring. They benefited from Lorie's own difficult experience as a youngster.

Our family made friends with welcoming couples on the street we were located on. Often when Jack and I went for an evening walk we were invited in for coffee. We were pleased that our children had playmates nearby. Chris and Lorie were happy to find a candy store just around the corner from our residence. On Saturday mornings it became routine for them to visit that store with some of their weekly allowances. The store keeper was pleasant and always greeted children with a big smile and a few kind words. Our two would return, each with a little brown bag, the contents of which were known only to one another. Back at home Chris and Lorie would be all smiles and giggles as they ran up to one of their bedrooms where they could be heard discussing which sweet they liked best and which ones they would consider trading. As children whose families moved from one community to another it was comforting for them to have one special place that they could count on being there on a regular basis. It was also a special time for brother and sister to bond, when sibling rivalry disappeared and when they became buddies as happy memories were made together, memories that neither would forget as they grew up and away from home.

****

After two years in Kamsack Jack got word that he would be transferred to a Staff-Sergeant's position in Prince Albert, the gateway to the Prince Albert National Park in north central Saskatchewan. Jack and I were very pleased with his well-deserved promotion, and once more I filled the children with positive thoughts about this new move. This would be our first city posting, and we knew Prince Albert would have more to offer than any smaller points. Added to our excitement was the fact that we would be purchasing our own house for the first time. And what a house it was! It was a four-level split on a nice lot with established lawn, trees, and shrubbery. We were in a pleasant residential area, and our house was next to a green space with a hill on it. We all had toboggan rides down that hill during the winters. Just over the hill was The John Diefenbaker School, so it was convenient for our youngsters. I accompanied the children to register for school the day after our arrival in the city. As we entered the school, Chris quickly sized up the method to be followed for registration. He offered to register himself while I helped with Lorie's registration. I was a little surprised, but since he seemed so confident, I agreed.

The three of us were finished in short order and soon on our way back home. We had not been in the house ten minutes when the doorbell rang. I was met at the door by a group of boys about Chris's age who were asking for Todd. My first reaction was to tell them they had the wrong house, but as I started to speak I caught sight of Chris on the second-level stairway. He was motioning to me and insistently pointing to himself. I went along with his intention and watched wordlessly as he walked across the kitchen where he greeted the boys, and off they went to get acquainted in the park. When he eventually returned home he rather sheepishly told me that he had registered himself as Todd which is his second name, and which, I learned for the first time, he much preferred to my long-held favourite name of Christopher. My own son with his twelve-year-old clever, crafty plans had fooled me. He did not offer any reason for taking his second name over his first, but I have suspicions he decided Todd was more masculine. After all, he'd never heard of a girl named Todd, although he knew a few called Chris. He has been known as Todd ever since, even though it took some time for his family to completely adjust. My mother never did call him anything but Chris; it was too difficult for her, and I suspect, she also preferred his first name.

Chris, now Todd, had wanted to take piano lessons a few years earlier, and although his interest faded after the first year, we still had the piano. It seemed sensible to now enroll Lorie in piano lessons. She went along with the idea at first, but it soon became clear that she was not very keen. Every practise session at home was stressful for both of us. After a reasonable trial I decided there was no sense in prolonging the misery, so Lorie's short piano career came to an ignominious end. Her talents lay elsewhere; she sensed it, and so did I. Luckily for Lorie, so did her grade six teacher, Mrs. Phyllis McKay, who recognized Lorie's natural artistic abilities. She praised and encouraged Lorie for each detailed illustration Lorie drew for homework assignments. Her friends were intrigued with her ability to sketch the likeness of people and things in their surroundings. She won a wildlife sponsored art contest with her illustration of wetland life. Her photo with the illustration appeared in the Prince Albert Herald Newspaper. With this encouragement, I registered Lorie at the Community College in an art course for young people.

As I drove Lorie to the weekly class, she looked forward to the assignments she would be given. She especially liked working on nature scenes, and although she was the youngest student there the instructor would sometimes hold her work up for the rest of the class to see. Lorie was always happy when I met her after class. That experience along with Mrs. McKay's support and praise gave Lorie an element of self-confidence. This was so important to a young girl who was so often the new kid on the block who had to prove her worth over and over at each new school, with every new group of young people she encountered. She quickly learned that art was not only her passion, but was the element that would introduce her and through which she could gain acceptance.

Jack's new position with the Force took him away from the city for days at a time. Besides inspecting Prince Albert City Detachment, he was flown by RCMP aircraft to inspect all Saskatchewan detachments north of Prince Albert. He saw a lot of beautiful and interesting country, but unfortunately he was, more often than not, gone all week. Even more difficult to deal with were the times that he and his pilot were snowed in at Buffalo Narrows or Uranium City, the weather too dangerous for flight. These occasions were great disappointments to me and to our children. We managed as best we could, but I knew that we were all robbed of precious time to be together as a family. We tried to compensate in various ways. We bought a white baby rabbit for Lorie and a gerbil for Todd. They had great fun with these new additions to our menagerie, and it filled some time for them as they showed these pets to their friends.

****

One winter day in 1972, I told the children that our Prime Minister, Mr. John Diefenbaker, would be in the city and that it was his home riding. He would be signing a new book at a downtown bookstore, and since their school was named for him, and because he was, after all, the prime minister, I felt they should be exposed to "His Greatness" even for a few moments. It was a snowy winter evening when I guided the car down the slippery slopes from our east-end home to the city's centre. By then, the children were primed for this momentous occasion. I bought a copy of Mr. Diefenbaker's book, *Those Things We Treasure*, for each of the children. I realized the subject matter would be of no interest to them at their tender ages, yet just meeting the author and having his signature on a book of their very own seemed important to me. We stood in line not quite sure what to expect. As we waited I heard some of the conversation the honoured man was having with a young father who was holding his baby of about one-year-old. As he admired the child, Mr. Diefenbaker said, "There is only one thing that Mrs. Diefenbaker and I regret, and that is that we never had children." I was struck with his sincerity with its undercurrent of sadness. His words served to remind me how very fortunate I was to have the gift of my two beautiful children. It never occurred to me that things would ever change. When it was our turn to meet Mr. Diefenbaker I was not only pleased to shake his hand, but to see him take Lorie's and Todd's hands in greeting. He spoke kindly and gently to them. Going back out into the wintry night, we were all aglow with a special feeling that had overtaken us. "See how lucky we are to be a family? Mr. Diefenbaker looked so sad when he was talking about not having a family". Lorie and Todd broke out in smiles as they nodded their heads. It had been a good evening for all three of us.

One year later and still in Prince Albert the children and I were to meet Mr. Diefenbaker once again, this time along with their dad who was to be presented with his RCMP long service medal by the great man. This ceremony to mark Jack's twenty years of faithful service to the Force was held in the reception room of Prince Albert's subdivision office. The children were proud of their dad and knew from our conversations at home that when a member of the RCMP was presented with a long service medal it was of great significance. It represented acknowledgement of his dedication and hard work as a member of Canada's National Police Force. As well, both our children looked forward to again seeing Mr. Diefenbaker who had made them feel so special at their first meeting.

After Mr. Diefenbaker posed with our family for a photo, and while the men were talking, Lorie quietly asked me, "May I take a picture to school? Everyone thinks I'm pretty lucky to meet such an important person". She was smiling broadly and her eyes were sparkling with anticipation. On this occasion Mr. Diefenbaker took the opportunity to speak to the children, one at a time, ignoring everyone else in the room for a few minutes, before turning to the other child with whom he spent equal time. He was kindly and personable, seeming genuinely interested in each child. Our family enjoyed tea or milk, and goodies with him that morning.

****

During the winters when Jack made it home for weekends we sometimes took the children out to Red River Park, just north of the city. Todd and Lorie skied on the gentle slopes there, and we all went for toboggan rides. We always looked forward to the hot chocolate and warm fireplace in the chalet. One New Year's Day when the chalet was closed we managed to make a fire in the park's outdoor pit where we cooked hot dogs on sticks. The children were in the sort of good mood they always displayed when we were on an outing that included the whole family as well as Toby, their spunky dog. The children laughed when we plunged the mustard and ketchup bottles in the snow where they stood ready for our buns. Then they ran off to chase one another in the woods. Toby was close behind. Their laughter and Toby's excited barking echoed back to us. When they were out of breath, they returned to the fire, ready to eat. We were all dressed well, so were comfortable even though we sat in the snow. I had hot drinks in thermos bottles. Toby enjoyed sniffing about in the woods, and catching bits of wieners that the children threw to him. We were surrounded by tall stands of pine and birch trees. It was snowing gently, and we all had snowflakes on our eyelashes. We had wanted our children to recognize that even the simplest family times could be special and meaningful. I knew that we were giving our youngsters another happy memory to store away with many others like traveling and camping trips, swimming and fishing trips, visits with grandparents, and so many other important times with our family.

In the fall we sometimes went for a ride through the forest north of Prince Albert. We loved to gaze down long driveways to isolated homes tucked into the woods. On these drives we would often see a deer or a fox, and any number of birds. We thought it would be wonderful to live in such a home with many opportunities to watch wildlife through the windows. I believe these experiences planted the seeds of nature awareness and were partly responsible for the many nature drawings and paintings Lorie would make in the years that followed. They show how deeply she loved nature. Eventually we built our own forest cottage, which has given us much joy and pleasure.

Nature never did betray the heart that loved her

—*William Wordsworth*

****

It was a sad fall day in 1974 when we discovered our much-loved Toby had been hit and killed by a car. Toby followed our car one pleasant September evening when Jack was driving Lorie's friend home. We were concerned when he did not return before we went to bed. Jack was leaving the city early the next morning. As the children left for school I started walking about calling Toby's name. When the children returned from school I enlisted their help. We asked friends and neighbors if they had seen Toby, but to no avail. At bedtime Lorie and Todd asked in worried tones what I thought had happened to their pet. Trying to reassure both them and myself, I answered, "Well, Toby is such a cute little guy and everyone loves him. I wouldn't be surprised if some children have not taken him home and he can't get out to come back. Anyway, I phoned the newspaper and put in an AD about his disappearance. Maybe someone who reads the AD will phone us. Let's just wait until tomorrow".

"I wish dad was at home", said a tearful Lorie.

"Me too," answered Todd in a raspy voice. I knew he was trying to be brave, just like I was trying.

As the children prepared to leave for school the next morning I reassured them that I would drive around to look for our pet. I started driving first in our part of the city before going further afield to areas I had never been before, hoping against hope that Toby had been picked up and that at the first opportunity he was attempting to find his way back home. At the supper table that evening both children looked pale and worried. I answered the phone on the first ring. Perhaps someone was responding to my AD. Someone was; it was a city employee who told me he had found Toby thrown up onto a lawn after being struck by a vehicle. He had just read our AD and knew the dog's identity by his license and veterinary tags. "I still have the collar tags and I can drop them off for you tomorrow."

The children could tell from my tone that the news was bad. As I turned to tell them I found them right in front of me. I slumped back against the wall as I gathered them both to me. "Toby was hit by a car. He died instantly," was all I could muster. Lorie and Todd broke down. We sobbed in one another's arms, wishing again that their dad was there with us. Supper was forgotten. We sat together on the living room sofa, trying to come to terms with this latest loss. It seemed so unfair that my youngsters had to face such a painful loss. They had already lost Kip and Blackie, our beloved family pets, and they had lost three homes with surroundings that had become familiar. They had had to leave their friends behind. They were without a father too much of the time, and now this. I was broken-hearted, but had to give my children all the comfort I could. That night we three slept together in my bed with Fancy, the cat, curled up at our feet.

****

That summer we travelled by train to Ontario where we visited with Jack's mother and his sisters in Sarnia. We visited Toronto and Niagara Falls and also toured about Parliament Hill in Ottawa. When we were passing the Prime Minister's residence I suggested we name our new pet Trudy, short for Trudeau. The children thought that was a good idea, and so the name stuck.

My niece was soon to be married in Regina, and we were all thrilled that she had invited Lorie, age twelve, to be her junior bridesmaid. Off to the dressmaker, down to the shoe store—life was fun. The dress was finished, hair was styled becomingly, and coaching in decorum and the part to be played as a bridal attendant was rehearsed a number of times. Dress rehearsal at our Prince Albert home recorded Lorie in her new yellow flowered dress and white shoes, white flower basket in hand, posing on the golden carpeted steps. At the wedding she played her part well, and we were very proud of her.

Being in the public eye at this large wedding gave Lorie a degree of confidence. Our relatives saw her in a different light other than a chubby shy child who liked to draw. Her new friends admired the photos showing Lorie in the wedding party; it was easy to see they were impressed. The important role that she carried out splendidly served as a first stepping stone which would confidently lead her to participation in many public events that were to follow in her teen years and into her young adult life.

We had lived in Prince Albert for three years; the children had made good friends and were doing well in school and other activities. There was only one thing missing from our lives, and that was having their dad more often present in our nice family home. We all mourned the lost time that had accumulated as the children grew up without his constant love and guidance. Jack and I talked about the situation, especially concerned that his superiors appeared to want him to continue in the same job. We reasoned that we had sacrificed three years; it was time for someone else to take over, relieving him for another position. We made the decision that he would request being relieved of his post in the north in favour of another placing so he could more regularly be at home. We decided we would go anywhere if it meant having a complete family most of the time. Still, it was our wish to remain in Prince Albert and have the children continue in their schools with their acquired friends. Instead of switching positions with a Prince Albert member of his rank and experience, which would require no transfer or resultant upheaval of families, the Force came up with an entirely different plan. The powers that be seemed to hear only one thing: we would go anywhere.

It was difficult to accept the Force's decision. We were being transferred to Swift Current in Southwest Saskatchewan. Todd, now fourteen, had just completed his first year at high school where he was happy with his teachers, friends, and sports teams. This move came as a blow to him, and he still readily admits it was the most difficult time of his young life. Lorie was also shaken, recognizing that she would once again be a stranger in a maze of students at the school she would be attending. The youngsters tried to handle the news since it was coupled with the fact that their dad would seldom be away from home. We were all sad to leave our lovely home and its neighbourhood.

We never did like the house we bought in Swift Current. It did not even have a garage. The house number 1113 seemed to bode ill. Apparently there was nothing available in that city comparable to our Prince Albert place. Perhaps we could make improvements, I had thought. One redeeming grace was that it was close to the schools our youngsters would be attending, and not far to Jack's office. I reluctantly gave in, and the purchase was made. We did make improvements and we made friends with a number of welcoming neighbours. We were to live in that house for thirteen years. It was from that home that, in turn Todd, then Lorie left for entire summers for summer jobs, and later, from where they left to begin their lives in academia. Lorie left from that place for the "time of her life", studying and working in Europe and London, England. That home would eventually see great unhappiness and much grief.

****

The first year at 1113 Jubilee Drive the youngsters tried valiantly to fit in to their new schools. After some time, Todd was slowly accepted by a few of his fellow classmates, and life improved for him once it became obvious what a keen sports competitor he was. He loved being on a midget hockey team. His dad was able to attend many of his games and drive him to hockey practise. His life was slowly coming together.

Lorie, at twelve, was taller than most girls her age, very blond, and light complexioned. When she arrived at her new school, she stood out from the regulars there, many of whom had gone to school together since kindergarten. Those youngsters had not had the experience of welcoming new students. Most did not do so. Soon Lorie discovered a girl her own age living on our street. Having just one friend in this strange community made all the difference. Dorothy, who had lived there all her life, was, nevertheless, not one of the 'in' crowd. She was a pleasant girl: tall, with lovely, smiling eyes. She and Lorie became fast friends, both excelling in basketball. Grace, a pretty girl of Chinese heritage, became their friend, and other girls were eventually added to their circle. These girls found strength in their own growing numbers; they no longer felt intimidated by the well established cliques.

Lorie joined Job's Daughters where her artistic talent was soon recognized. She was confirmed at St. Stephens Anglican Church we attended in Swift Current. Reverend Ivor Ottery was a mild mannered gentleman with a deep faith. He had a lot of empathy for people experiencing problems. Our family grew to love and respect him, and admired him and his wife for the wonderful care they gave their two young sons, both of whom were stricken with muscular dystrophy. These nice looking boys attended services and went to school in their wheelchairs, and although they were obviously disabled, they always had smiles for anyone speaking to them.

During confirmation classes, Lorie felt a sort of bond develop between her and our minister. She must have sensed his understanding of her insecurity being the new girl in town. One day, as Lorie and I were hurrying toward the shopping mall exit, we caught sight of Ivor coming in, and we smiled and waved to one another. Lorie touched my arm and said, "Mom, did you notice the aura surrounding Rev. Ottery's head?" Somewhat taken aback, I quickly turned to spot Ivor in the crowd, and then answered, "Ah— no I didn't. Did you see something?"

Lorie had a faraway look as she quietly answered, "Yah, I did. There was definitely a light around his head, like an aura."

"Well, he's such a special person, I expect if anyone has an aura it would be him." As we drove home, Lorie was unusually quiet, obviously in deep thought. Ivor was the special person our family would come to turn to when tragedy would befall us.

It would become evident particularly during her university years that Lorie struggled with religion and faith. She questioned and searched as she saw validity in religions other than just Christianity. Divisions within the Christian faith also troubled her. She believed faith to be what spoke to one's heart, so to her it was not important which religion one embraced. She accepted Christ into her life and spoke openly, especially the last year of her life, of her guardian angel that she believed watched over her.

A letter from a university friend:
    Dear Lorie…I know how you are feeling right now. Well, listen. It doesn't matter how many times you've attended 'such and such' a church or whether you're accepted by that church. What is important is that you have asked God to take over and come into your life. Just once will do it; you don't gain his acceptance by repeating your beliefs and going to church regularly. God loves you and has a great plan for you. He wants to be with you and show his love to you. You are a very beautiful person He has created and that shows through in your 'aura'. Have a good day, eh and remember that if you even just think about Him and talk to Him silently and remember Him all day while life guarding, partying, jogging, laughing—that is prayer. It doesn't have to be knees down, hands folded, pious thoughts all the time. What a rush, eh. God bless you.

Love in Christ, Robb

But while still a growing teenager at home, Lorie excelled in swimming and obtained lifeguard and swimming instructor badges. At age thirteen she modeled two garments in a fashion show for which I acted as mistress of ceremonies. This 1975 event was held to entertain RCMP wives of members who played in the first annual hockey tournament that Jack had organized along with the Kinsmen Club. Monies raised went to local sports for youth in Swift Current and area. The RCMP was an ever-present influence in all our lives.

I was hopeful that Lorie would eventually learn to play a musical instrument. When she showed an interest in flute music we wasted no time in finding a teacher, then purchased a beautiful silver flute. But her main passion remained in art. It was evident to teachers and students alike that Lorie had an uncanny gift in her ability to draw. Her school assignments requiring illustrations stood out among her classmates. Also, a crowd would often be attracted to wherever she might be drawing likenesses of other students or teachers. Her cartoon figures brought her praise and admiration. Anyone needing a poster turned to Lorie for fresh and innovative drawings. The next year Lorie was awarded with the school's Best Artist Prize, which gave her two summer weeks of art studies at Fort Qu'Appelle's Art School. She enjoyed it so much that we enrolled her for the following summer. Lorie enthusiastically gave herself over to total involvement, churning out her creativity into piece after piece of bold brightness. When she ran out of supplies she did not hesitate to pull a sheet off her bed; the sheet was quickly transformed into a 5' x 8' batik of cheerful sunflowers which soon, after being stretched onto a frame, covered most of one wall in our dining room. She was thrilled to have her talent recognized and to have her reputation raised. It was wonderful to see our Lorie a happy girl once more.

****

Difficult days still lay ahead. Nine-thirty on the evening of August 26, 1975 stands out in our memory. We had lived in Swift Current only one year when Jack was struck down by a drunk driver on a remote stretch of #13 Highway in the southwest corner of Saskatchewan. At twilight he had stopped to assist a woman who appeared to be having motor difficulties. With his head inside the car's hood, he was concentrating on the repair job he was attempting so both he and the woman could get home that night. A car, driven by a habitual drinker, came swerving toward them at great speed, and crushed Jack between the parked police car and the woman's car. The result was Jack almost bleeding out at the scene, then eventually being airlifted to University Hospital in Saskatoon where he had emergency surgery that night, followed by many other surgeries, much pain, and long rehabilitation. His life and ours have never been the same. He suffers pain and disability still.

I had to explain to our youngsters, then about twelve and fifteen, what had happened to their dad. They grew up fast that night. I made a frantic call to my aged mother to see if she could come to be with the family for a few days, spoke to a neighbour, asking her to keep a watch over them that night, and asked another neighbour to drive me to the local airport. I flew to Saskatoon with Jack when he arrived by road ambulance. I knew his condition was critical. The nightmare begun that night continued on for Jack and our family for many months to come.

What a responsibility I had to place on the shoulders of our young son when I left him in charge of the household each time I raced back to Jack's side in another city. What fear he must have felt about the present and the future for his dad, himself and for all of us. What pain it must have caused when I told him that he would have to drop out of football trials. How unfair it all was.

How frightened and lonely our Lorie must have been. What dreadful images must have played out in her fertile imagination. She was still adjusting to this new location. We were strangers in this new place. She needed her mother while her dad needed me more. This was all too much to expect of a young girl, entirely too much.

Somehow we muddled on for several months before Jack was able to travel back home, albeit with full-length casts on both legs. I dealt with all the problems entailed in the home with one so incapacitated. I saw to our children's needs, and they helped me with chores as well as attending to their homework. Looking back on all of that I often wonder how we managed. The youngsters were eventually able to spend more time with their friends and to indulge in their own interests. But, I believe this whole episode scarred them both and skewed their development off its normal course. As if life had not been unkind enough.

****

In the spring of 1976, Jack still had partial casts on both legs. To relieve his boredom and inactivity I suggested we attend an auction mart to be held on June 3. It had been a lovely day; there was no wind and the sky was still clear and sunny when I drove him to the mart on the western outskirts of Swift Current. We chose a seating area that provided him with a lot of leg room, and where Jack was enjoying the conversations and activity around us, the auctioneer's loudspeaker call. After almost two hours of constant noise in the windowless building I happened to notice the large sliding doors beside us where drifting inward. When a young man stood to put his hands on the doors I could tell it took some force to hold them in place. I wondered about that. In moments rain started to pelt down on the metal roof. The lights went out and a forceful wind suddenly was upon the building. The large doors cracked apart and blew in as parts of the ceiling broke away. A timber struck me on the head and knocked me to the floor; debris continued to fall on me.

People panicked and scrambled for the nearest exit. Jack helped me to my feet and I lead him to the opening nearby. Our way was obstructed with fallen timbers and other lumber. We struggled to get footing, slipping and sliding with every step. Finally we were outside in the utter darkness and pelting rain driven by a frightening and powerful wind. People crowded past us, many calling out for their family members, their voices lost in the tornado's howling. We sought shelter behind a pile of lumber. I remember it was difficult to breathe as the wind tore at my face. Then I felt something hanging between my eyes; I felt it and with the next flash of lightning I saw blood on my hand.

It seemed we waited for a very long time for the storm to abate or for someone to come to our aid. Finally lights from an ambulance showed through from a distance. I kept calling out that my husband had two broken legs and needed help. Eventually we were taken to an ambulance and attendants assisted us inside. Traversing rivers of water across many streets, the driver was able to pull up to the hospital's emergency entrance. As I continued to babble about Jack having two broken legs all hands came to his aid. I asked one of the nurses to phone our home to make sure our children were safe. I was wonderfully relieved that they were fine and that we had made it to safety where Jack was receiving medical attention. Soon I had my vital signs checked and wounds sutured. It was determined that since I had a head injury I would have to remain in hospital at least overnight. Jack's soaked casts were replaced so he could return home. Again our good neighbours came to our family's aid.

Our children had to hear once again that their dad, but now also their mother, had been in an accident. Their young lives had been returning to usual routine in recent months. They had both their parents safely at home with them. Their dad was slowly improving and they had been making plans for the time when he would be free of casts and eventually getting back to normal. Now this. They were relieved when their dad came home later that night, told them their mom was okay, but just had to stay in hospital for a few days as a precaution. When I returned home the children, only a little surprised at my bruised and sutured forehead and ear, greeted me with hugs and with a newspaper clipping from the *Regina Leader Post*. It described the devastating tornado that had ripped through Swift Current, leaving two people hospitalized. The children giggled, telling me I was now famous having my name in the news. It was good to hear them having a little fun after the fright they had recently experienced. Jack, with his legs elevated in his recliner, smiled at his family. Trudy, our dog was dancing around me and even Fancy, our cat arched her back against my legs. It was so good to be at home.

****

Lorie went on to attend the city's comprehensive high school in 1977, the same year that Todd was in his last year before graduation. When an evening drafting class was offered Lorie and her dad enrolled together, enjoying this time of shared interest. At a time when few youngsters wore dental braces, it was deemed a requirement for Lorie. Since there was no orthodontist practising in Swift Current it was necessary to make the three-hour drive to Regina each month. As it happened, a decade later, her brother became Swift Current's orthodontist, regularly driving there from his main clinic in Calgary. Lorie's braces were a trial for her, giving her frequent pain physically and emotionally. She had just begun to use a little makeup, and she took care to keep her always-beautiful hair well kempt. She took a babysitting course, and used her money for some makeup, a few clothes, and incidentals.

Lorie enjoyed her school's sports events, and she always did well in sports day competitions. Running cleared her mind of any concerns or worries she had, and it gave her the exercise she needed whenever she was spending a lot of time concentrating on art projects. While in Grade ten she applied for, and was accepted as, a lifeguard at a motel pool very close to our home. Several other girls, especially from the unfriendly set, coveted this position. They were outraged that a new girl would take the position over long-time residents. A couple of the meanest girls tried to intimidate Lorie whenever they would find her alone. They called her names and insulted her. This was very difficult for Lorie, but she persevered knowing that she had been hired on her ability and not by leaning on a well-known city name. The catty girls were unrelenting, always looking for new fodder to use on this upstart in their midst.

Lorie had longed for the day when she could have her braces removed. When that day came she was thrilled and very relieved. Her smile was becoming, the difficult treatment having proved worthwhile. She had a few wonderful weeks of feeling free and fully alive. She smiled and laughed a lot at home and with her friends who helped her rejoice. The unfriendly girls must have felt threatened by the natural beauty of this tall, lithesome girl with the lovely smile and long, blond curly hair. They seemed to resent her.

I had noticed that Lorie's spine had developed a slight curve, but since she was a growing girl, thought it would correct itself in time. When it did not, I had our physician examine her. He diagnosed the condition as scoliosis (which I had been hoping it was not), and advised that there was no alternative but to have her fitted for a body brace that she would have to wear for about two years. Of all the bad news and difficult times Lorie had experienced during her fifteen years, this was the cruelest. When she heard the news I could see she was devastated. Later, when she saw the grotesque apparatus that was to become a part of her, I could tell she was drowning in pain.

I suggested to Lorie that we go shopping to find some new outfits; ones that would accommodate both her and the brace. It was a tall order. Shopping with a teenage girl can be a trying, even hopeless task at the best of times. After much persistence we managed to find a few articles that would accomplish some of what we had hoped. The only physical relief Lorie was afforded was when she could daily escape from the brace for a long, soaking tub bath. After that I would massage her tender pressure areas and apply talcum powder. It was a very trying period as I did my best to alleviate my daughter's unwarranted load. How brave she was to venture out the door that first morning on her way to school. I knew it took every scrap of determination she could muster. I can only imagine the stares, people's reactions, comments and questions. Also, I feared from past experience that some girls would make Lorie's trial even more difficult. My beautiful daughter came home, inwardly battered and bruised, just wanting to be left alone. Her friends, however, stayed with her and did their best to lift her spirits.

Lorie immersed herself in artwork. Her artistic abilities were becoming well known by teachers and students of the comprehensive high school. Her art teacher was pleased to have such a talented student in his classes, and he encouraged her. It was during this period of her life that Lorie began to show her work in competitions and shows. Soon her dad was making frames in which to accommodate increasing pieces of Lorie's work. He often drove her and her creations to shows in other communities. Her work placed high in every competition resulting in sales of some pieces and requests for others. At the young age of sixteen she was commissioned to do an oil painting scene of an individual's homestead. She also worked tirelessly doing works in pointillism, a form her high school art teacher, Paul Rezansoff, had recently introduced her to. Pointillism was invented in the late 1800s by Georges Seurat in Paris. This technique involves methodically placing dots of color in specific ways to create shadow, highlights and figures. She was intrigued with this new way of creating art, and although it is very time consuming and requires great precision she created several works using this method. We encouraged her to have two of her pointillism pieces made into hasty notes. We were so proud to do this for her, and to put samples on display in a few specialty shops in Swift Current and area. This extra income would help with expensive purchases of art supplies, of canvass, paints, brushes and all the accoutrement that accompanies artwork. Just as importantly, it would put her name out there and give her self-confidence.

When Lorie entered a provincial art competition, she was thrilled and honoured to have her pointillism work purchased by the Saskatchewan government and have it travel the province for showings. This winning picture was a collection of hanging cooking pots. After the picture had toured for one year, Lorie decided to donate it along with her photo to the Swift Current Public Library, housed in the same building as the art gallery.

Lorie was used to being called upon by teachers and students alike when an artistic touch was required for posters or special signage. When in grade ten she created a charming but simplistic piece for the graduating class. She painted two yellow daisy blossoms with a couple of petals just beginning to fall from one. The centre of the flower features a butterfly drawn with lifelike detail. The text below the picture announces, "We may never pass this way again."

That framed original of more than thirty years ago, and protected by glass, hangs in our home still. How often I longingly gaze at that sentiment, and how prophetic is the echo of those words.

There are echoes still of its star artist at the Swift Current Comprehensive High School. With Lorie as the driving force, she and other students produced a mural on a long wall of the second floor just above the main entrance. The mural, cleverly divided in the middle, accurately depicts life on Swift Current's Main Street in its early beginnings, with the other half showing the street and buildings with its cars and signs as it was in 1980, the year of the painting. A brass plaque announces the name of the artist and her helpers.

Many years later when Swift Current became a satellite orthodontic practise for Lorie's brother, Todd, he one day had a call from a teacher he had known during high school. The teacher explained that during renovations in the art department, two charcoal drawings by Lorie had surfaced. It seemed the pieces had slipped behind a cupboard and were only revealed during renovations. He thought Todd would like to have them, so he delivered them to Todd's clinic. We were a bit overcome by this surprising, deja vous discovery that we welcomed into our home as if it was a longed-for letter from our dear girl. The two scenes come from Lorie's memories of Goodsoil and the neighbouring Meadow Lake Provincial Park. One depicts a forest scene done in the vibrant green of spruce trees. The second, contrasting piece, is a typical burnout scene showing the trees standing tall, black and naked. After overcoming our shock of seeing these new pieces and adding them to our large collection of Lorie's work, her dad and I had them placed behind glass and framed. They hang in our home, long a personal art gallery of Lorie's work. Anyone showing an interest in work in the entrance hall or beyond is given a tour of all the hangings upstairs and down. It is our great pride to do this. We think Lorie would approve.

Lorie's long awaited unveiling took place when, after eighteen months in which she developed necessary perseverance and a modicum of patience, her body brace was removed for the last time. Her still developing body had corrected the slight curve to her spine. She could now face the world on equal footing. Out went accommodating clothes, in came new slim fitting designs; flirting became a possibility; dates became a reality. Dancing was fun again; skiing, running, swimming were all renewed joys for her. As a nurse and as her mother I was concerned about fad diets Lorie was adopting. I explained to her that with a healthy diet and exercise her weight would, with time, normalize. At the same time I understood her position that she had had no control over her life for so long that she just wanted to handle this area on her own. It was difficult for me to watch her rigidly restricting her caloric intake; she seemed to be trying to bury her pain of the brace days. But eventually she leveled out at a weight she was happier with. I relaxed when she returned to healthier meals.

Our daughter was still busy trying to make up for lost time when graduation loomed large. She would have to settle into studies if she was to be admitted to university. She had to decide what universities to apply to, and then send application forms. Lorie waited to hear if she would be hired as a lifeguard at the Cypress Hills Provincial Park, the same park that her brother had worked at the previous two summers. There were clothing choices to be made for special graduation events. She had to decide whom to invite as her grad escort. Everything was happening so fast. She was emotionally unprepared, and she floundered.

Everything came together, but just barely. Lorie's escort was a fairly new acquaintance from another town. He was tall, (a prerequisite in a date for her height), dark and quite good looking. This was the ace up her sleeve when all the girls were anxious to know which girl was going with which boy. Only her close friends were confidants, while all others were taken by surprise to see that Lorie and her secret date made quite a handsome couple. Elsie and Cliff Wilson arrived from Vancouver to see Lorie graduate. Elsie was ecstatic to see how Lorie had grown into such a lovely young woman—Lorie, the little girl who once loved to visit her, sometimes with a basket of kittens. Lorie was happy to see her friend once again.

At the awards event just prior to graduation, Lorie was the recipient of an art scholarship. We have a favourite photo of her with her good buddy, Dorothy, both holding awards, following the event. There were art assignments to be finished and much cramming to be done those last days before final exams. The pace quickened as Lorie tried to accomplish as much as possible every day, and sometimes, into the night. She was pleased to receive a letter accepting her into the lifeguard position for the summer. Once exams were over she had a few short days to spend with her good friends, and to prepare for her move away from home not only for the first time, but also for two whole months. She needed to apply for a room in residence at University of Saskatchewan where she was enrolled in the Fine Arts Program. By staying up late for several nights, Lorie was able to attend to all these matters on time. She was always much like her dad in this respect—both had always taken on a seemingly impossible load of responsibilities, never concerned about deadlines. She followed her dad's lead by staying with work projects until their completion.

Her summer job provided housing shared with several other girls, so that was one less concern. Meals were another matter. Each girl was responsible for providing and cooking her own food. Most times the girls lived on fruit, sandwiches and pasta dishes, all suitable for the short term, but a steady diet of grab-what-is-handy was not healthy. They also, too often, sacrificed sleep so they could enjoy this newfound freedom by partying with the boys on staff. Lorie had worked very hard at school so she deserved some fun, and we knew we had to let her make her own decisions. We were proud of her lifesaving skills when she told us how she had saved the life of a swimmer while on duty as the lifeguard. At the end of summer when Lorie came home exhausted and a few pounds heavier, she slept long hours for two or three days. She was happy to be on a healthier diet, and she soon returned to her regime of daily runs. She spent her days organizing her wardrobe and shopping with her friends in preparation for university. Those were the best of times—she had survived the summer job and was back home with us and her friends, and yet the time was overshadowed by concerns: She would soon be leaving us all and would be facing a whole new experience with strangers. Naturally, she was having a few qualms about the future. Todd was completing his first degree at the U of S when Lorie started there. She listened to his experiences with great interest as she had always looked up to him. Unfortunately, none of her friends would be attending the U of S.

The day we drove her into Saskatoon, Lorie was quiet and anxious. Once we located her room and helped carry in her bags, it became obvious that she did not want us to linger. She did not wish to appear needy in view of other students. We obliged, knowing she had to sort things out for herself: looking over the campus plan, finding her way to classes and the cafeteria and studying the city bus routes. For most students, especially those from out of town, there were many trials and errors, but Lorie grew to love her classes and soon became a favourite of her professors. She made new friends, and became better acquainted with other students she had barely known in Swift Current. Those four years were filled with studies, working on art projects, university activities, and parties. After the first year, Lorie was ready to move out of residence and into a small apartment that she would share with a couple of friends. From the time she had left home her dad and I prayed daily for her health, protection, safety and happiness. Never quite satisfied with her appearance, Lorie had secretly planned to have a "nose job" once she was settled in Saskatoon. When she phoned to tell us of her plans she assured us that her roommate and good friend, Loran, would look after her. So she had her nose cropped slightly, and after the bruising left, Loran and Lorie conspired about taking "after" pictures. Loran, who was taking a university photography class, took glamour photos of Lorie. We have always been so grateful for those photos showing Lorie so happy and looking quite glamorous with just the right touch of makeup, and her shimmering, gorgeous, long hair. If she was happy with the slight change to her appearance, then we were happy for her.

One weekend when Lorie was at home, she was out in my aging white Chevy with a few of her girlfriends. They had a wonderful time catching up as they drove around Swift Current. Suddenly, they noticed there were flames coming out of the engine. The girls were all shocked. Lorie stopped the car, and all the girls jumped out, horrified by what was happening. They phoned me from a nearby house. Her dad picked them up, and later he had the vehicle checked out by a mechanic. He could find nothing wrong with the engine, and since I had never had any trouble with the car, we were all mystified. I pondered, silently, at the exceptional difficulties that had befallen Lorie throughout much of her life. Perhaps I was overreacting, but the subject remained in my mind. Another occasion found Lorie at the wheel of my Chevy when she and some girl friends were touring about Swift Current. Somehow (we never fully understand how) the car slipped off the road into the ditch at a railway crossing. While all the girls got out of the car to study their dilemma a train passed them several times shuffling railcars onto sidings. It happened that the engineer plainly saw the girls' problem. To their amazement the train stopped, and a couple of men from the train approached the scene carrying a lengthy chain. Without ceremony they pulled the car out of the ditch and grinned broadly as Lorie and her friends tried to express their appreciation. In minutes the girls were on their way, talking about their fright as well as overwhelming relief at, and appreciation for, the kindness shown to them. Lorie's belief in guardian angels was strengthened that day.

****

One winter I phoned Lorie to say I had bought her a secondhand fur coat in good condition. She sounded very pleased, as she had found waiting at bus stops in Saskatoon had proven cold and uncomfortable. Her dad would be going into the city that week, so he made arrangements to take the coat and meet Lorie for dinner. That winter evening at *The Keg* on Saskatoon's Eighth Street was a memorable

time for father and daughter. It was a wonderful time for
Lorie to have her dad all to herself, and it was Jack's great
pleasure to treat his only daughter. She was very pleased
with the fur coat, so we were all happy.

We received this postcard written between Lorie's
second year at U of S and before her summer job began at
Cypress Hills Provincial Park:

~~~~~~~~~~~~~~~~~~~~~~~

Banff, AB.

May 26/82

Dear Mom and Dad, Guess where I am—Banff!
Heidi and I came for two days to ski before the
season ends! We camped one night (in a tent and
it snowed!) and one night we stayed at Dot's in the
"Hat." It's beautiful here—skiing was fantastic. I
didn't have to spend much money either. I'll have
to tell you about the crazy things that happened
here. (For instance, we got stranded on the highest
mountain in Sunshine. The chair lift broke down!
The ski patrollers had to get us down). All for
now—Love, Lorie

P.S. Have a good Holiday!

~~~~~~~~~~~~~~~~~~~~~~~

During the spring of 1982 Lorie had some time at home
before reporting for her summer job. She had her heart set
on buying a surf sail, and when friends told her of a part time
job working with a landscaper she immediately applied for
it. She had envisioned planting and watering plants; reality
had her spading up large areas for new flowerbeds as well
as loading soil and fertilizer into and out of a wheelbarrow.
Each evening after she arrived home exhausted and with

sore muscles, she had a long soapy tub bath. Although Lorie was disillusioned with the job, she was determined to stay with it until she earned the thousand dollars she needed for the surf sail. Her dad and I were proud of her. We also shared in her pleasure the day we accompanied her to make this special purchase. She happily mastered this new sport in the small lake at Cypress Hills Provincial Park.

Lorie, her dad and I were excited when Todd and Kim, both U of S grads, became engaged. Lorie was pleased when they asked her to be one of their bridesmaids. When the big day arrived Todd and Kim looked charming in their formal wedding attire. Lorie was lovely in her maroon bridesmaid dress topped with frothy white lace, identical to ones worn by Kim's sister and a girlfriend. With all eyes on her, Lorie confidently carried out her duties of lighting ceremonial candles during the church service. I wondered if she then recalled, as I did, her first experience as a bridal attendant. My two sisters and their husbands as well as my mother and some of our good friends were in attendance. It was a proud moment for me, attired in a mother-of-the-groom long dress, and for Jack in a smart new suit, when we entered the church and walked passed all these friends and relatives, to take our places in a front pew. After the service there were many hugs and handshakes, much smiling and laughter. As we cheered the wedding party off for a formal photographic session in the park, we slowly made our way to the reception hall. When the wedding party appeared they formed a reception line so each guest could greet the newlyweds and their attendants. A grand meal followed with tinkling glasses demanding the groom kiss his bride over and over. A dance capped the festivities. I was pleased to have a dance with my son while Jack took Kim for a whirl, and I could see Lorie laughing as she danced with one or two of the groomsmen. It was altogether a special day and evening for our whole family. Lorie's gift to Todd and Kim was a large package of Thank You hasty-notes with the image of roses that she had laboriously created with the pointillism technique she had perfected. This very personal gift was a labor of love, her love and admiration for her brother and her pleasure at having a "sister."

During the afterglow of the day I looked forward to someday seeing Jack walk our girl down the aisle. What a picture that would be! Lorie would look gorgeous on her dad's arm, the two of them tall and handsome with curly blond hair. Their eyes would be sparkling with joy, and they would be smiling. The groom would likely be handsome, tall and dark. He would be an architect or from another profession. They would have met at university.

The art students were used to being viewed by others as "artsy," a term intended as a put-down. By the time four years had passed and convocation was looming, the art students had decided they would play out their nickname to the fullest. Since all art students would be having a showing of their work at the university's Snelgrove Art Gallery followed by a reception, they decided to opt out of the regular convocation exercises, and to put all their energy into the art show. They had chosen to receive their degrees without ceremony to further set themselves apart from the rest of the student body. Plans were made some weeks in advance, during which each student decided what outrageous, "artsy" attire he or she would wear. Lorie chose a brilliant blue suede dress that a friend made for the occasion. The dress was very short and was cinched in by a wide belt with a large decorative buckle. Her long, shapely legs were encased in pantyhose of the same colour, and she wore heels to match the belt. As the piece de resistance, sections of her long, curly hair had been sprayed with brilliant blue coloring. She dramatically accentuated her large, luminous blue eyes with dark eyeliner and blue eye shadow. She looked smashing, everyone in the art gallery turned to get a better view. Her look of determination was plain to everyone, as if she was saying, "You want artsy? I'll give you artsy." Her message seemed to emit from every pore.

Even though her gallery fellows all dressed according to the plan, Lorie stood out as the star. Although we knew about the special costume, her dad and I were not prepared for the dramatics of make-up and especially the blue hair spray. We were a little taken aback but did not show it as we supported her and her fellows in their decision. However, we did notice a couple of guests roll up their eyes, as they made no attempt at concealing their disapproval. After digesting the event, I could better understand Lorie's purpose, and grew to be proud of her attempt to shock people so they might come to understand that she and her fellows were serious artists, and that they, and their work, were not to be dismissed easily. We had looked forward to her convocation and were disappointed that Lorie and her classmates would not be on stage to receive their degrees. But with time we understood their rationale, and from then on I would find myself occasionally chuckling about how the young artists had pulled it off. Lorie had acquired her degree in Fine Arts, and her dad and I also took pride in the scholarship that she won at that time.

> "Art, as far as it is able, follows nature, as a pupil imitates his master; thus your art must be, as it were, God's grandchild."
>
> —Dante, Inferno, Canto XI

Lorie was incredulous that a few of her friends were starting to get married. She was concerned that they had not completed their education and would not go on to further experiences before marrying. Gamely acting as bridesmaid for a couple of her friends, she never lost sight of all that she wanted to do, to attain, to experience. She tried to accept that not everyone saw life on such a grand scale, but she never wavered from her ideals. She seemed to know she had so much to pack into her life.

During the last year at the U of S, Lorie weighed in her mind which scholastic route to take once she had her first degree. She studied programs from other universities, UBC (University of British Columbia) and U of A (University of Alberta) which seemed likely choices. She wanted to pursue a degree in architecture. She felt drawn to UBC, and her application was accepted there. She also received a favourable reply from U of A, and was intrigued by the offer of a part-time instructor position in the Arts department there. Decisions, decisions,what to do? After some agonizing, Lorie chose UBC, and at that moment her fate was sealed.

If only she had not attended UBC, or if only she had not qualified to do "studies abroad", had not decided to stay in London after studies in Athens, had not readily been accepted at an architectural firm…there are no ends to "if only."

During the summers Lorie had returned to work at Cypress Hills, but after convocation she wanted a change. She worked for the Red Cross Water Safety Program with headquarters in Regina. Before going to this new job, we had her at home with us for a couple of weeks at the end of classes. Again, she tried to normalize her chaotic eating habits, which came with all the responsibilities she had to deal with as a student and balancing that with her social life. She also got into a routine of morning runs.

Her job involved driving a Red Cross car to several communities throughout the province to familiarize swimming instructors with the Red Cross programs and to ensure they closely followed the program. My mother and sister lived in Regina, so it was good for us to know she had family there. Lorie had her heart set on attending a summer art school north of Prince Albert at Emma Lake, a school that is an extension of the art program at the U of S. By planning an intensive work schedule she was able to have a week off to attend this school. Lorie was ecstatic at not only being able to land the summer job, but as well, to have time to go to Emma Lake. I once more saw signs of our daughter overloading herself, and I prayed she would be able to pull this off unscathed.

It was always a sight to see her preparing for a trip. She would scoop up an armful of clothing from her room and drop things onto the back seat of the car. Packing took too much time and she never had enough of that! Off she went in my trusty Chevrolet. She thoroughly enjoyed being a part of that program working alongside seasoned older artists. She worked long hours producing wonderful large pieces in acrylic paint. Those same pieces are appreciated and commented on by everyone visiting our home.

Leonardo da Vinci asks an interesting question in one of his notebooks: "Why does the eye see a thing more clearly in dreams than the imagination when awake? One answer is that the eye of the soul perceives the eternal realities so important to the heart. In waking life, most of us see only with our physical eyes, even though we could, with some effort of imagination, glimpse fragments of eternity in the most ordinary passing events. Dream teaches us to look with that other eye, the eye that in waking life belongs to the artist, to each of us as artist."

As Lorie made plans to move to Vancouver, I consoled myself with the fact that our dear friend, Elsie, lived there. She would be only too happy to *mother hen* our girl given the opportunity. It was good for Lorie to know she had a good friend to count on in this strange, new, and larger city. She lived in residence for a few months, but when she became friends with a young divorced woman from the School of Architecture, she was happy to move in with Marnie and her two school age children. They all became fast friends. Lorie used her bike to get back and forth to school, but upon hearing her stories of close escapes in heavy traffic, we urged her to take the bus. The School of Architecture was a small school, her class consisting of about a dozen students, so they became a close-knit family. Lorie was popular in her class, and she made good friends. Her letters and phone calls seemed to be reassuring. We started to relax for the first time since seeing her off to this more distant city.

Lorie was thrilled to be given a summer job researching heritage buildings in B.C. She travelled with another girl from her college to the sites of these buildings at Fort Steele and to St. Andrews Cathedral in Victoria. She likely chose the Fort Steele location because the RCMP had always been a strong influence in her life. She was also drawn to the beauty of cathedrals. The girls photographed the buildings and did detailed, painstaking scale drawings. We knew Lorie was dedicated to her work, and one time when we were talking about it, she exclaimed enthusiastically, "Just *wait* 'til you see the house I'm going to build *you!*"

Lorie's first experience with the construction of a building had come when she was about fifteen. I have a vivid memory of her on hands and knees helping me to pound nails into our cottage floor along a line Jack had penciled out for us. The sky was summer blue with soft white, fluffy clouds skidding overhead, and all around us, before the walls were built, were fluttering green aspen leaves and swaying pine boughs. Lorie enthusiastically pounded away, feeling the excitement with us of having our very own lake cottage in the Meadow Lake Provincial Park. We were working together as a family, and Lorie did not see the work she contributed as a burden, but rather as a joyous occasion. It gave her a sense of pride to know she was helping bring about our family's dream. It meant so much to her dad and I to witness her positive attitude. That experience brought us even closer together. Another memory is of Lorie sitting on the mattress on the bare floor of her upstairs bedroom in the partially finished cottage. She had just built from scraps of building material, a small box that held her mirror, hairbrush, and a few cosmetics. Jack and I chuckled at how her first building experience had inspired her to create this little box, but we knew she did it with pleasure and satisfaction. That small incident demonstrated to us Lorie's initiative and persistence. It made us feel proud. Where the stairs would eventually be was a ladder built firmly onto the wall. None of us thought of this as a hardship, but only one part of the unfolding of the longed for cottage. Lorie was excited enough just thinking of summer holidays at the lake that she invited her good friend, Dorothy, to spend some time with us at the cottage even in its unfinished state.

We cherish the picture of Lorie sitting on the cottage fireplace hearth. She had just come in from cross-country skiing and had hurried to the warmth of the fire. I took the photo before she had removed her toque and jacket; her cheeks are rosy, and she is smiling. This photo remains on a wall at the cottage. Little did any of us know this would be her last visit to her beloved cottage. Although her summer jobs were often with the provincial parks, she was unable to be located at or near Meadow Lake Provincial Park. Every winter she was away at school.

****

In 1985 we shared the news with Todd and Lorie that their dad and I planned to build and operate a miniature golf course in the park not far from our cottage. We had decided to have this small summer business ready by the time we retired. We gave Lorie the ideas we had in mind and asked her if she could draw up plans that we might be able to use. She was at UBC at that time and very immersed in studies and assignments, but she stayed up late several times to complete the work for us. We felt badly when she later revealed to us her heavy schedule. She was relieved when the job was completed, but she was also overjoyed to demonstrate to her parents what she was capable of, and of how much she wanted to help us; how much she loved us. The drawings were professionally done and showed acute attention to detail. We were awed to see the artistry in our girl's work, but unfortunately she had envisioned a grander scale for our project than we had intended. Because of that we were pained to acknowledge that we were not able to use her drawings.

Excerpt of a letter Lorie wrote to her grandmother:

~~~~~~~~~~~~~~~~~~~~~~~

Happy Valentine's Day! Feb. 10/85

Dear Grandma—Hi there! Thanks so much for the money for the San Francisco trip. I am really looking forward to a much needed change of pace. Because it is part of a class, I don't anticipate a "Holiday", but I'm sure I'll have a fun time. School is hard. I work hard and it seems to be paying off. I had a major critique the other day and I received a first class (A). I was up all the night before finishing the drawings of the building I designed. I was almost too tired to be happy. It's worth it though. I'm glad to be doing this—I expected it to be like this—so I'm not surprised. There are good times every once in a while but I'm really here for the school. This summer I will hopefully get a good job so I can "afford" next year better than I am doing this year. Next year I have a chance to study in Greece (I think I told you this before). Anyway, it sure will take a lot of work (for marks) and work (for money) and work (to organize the trip). It's not easy getting an education these days! How are Janie and the baby? Say Hi to everyone in Regina (Marj and the boys).

Love, Lorie

~~~~~~~~~~~~~~~~~~~~~~~~

Lorie received this letter of commendation for her excellent work at her summer job in British Columbia:

Dear Lorie: I was pleased to receive your final results for this summer's Student Employment Program project. The quality of the work you completed was excellent and without question met our expectations. The heritage program of Fort Steele and St. Andrew's Cathedral will certainly benefit from your efforts. Let me commend you for successfully carrying out this project. An annotated bibliography of the reports and results of the 1982–1985 Student Employment Program projects is being prepared. The bibliography is an exciting project because it provides an opportunity to present the accomplishments of the many valuable heritage projects undertaken in the past four years. We are looking forward to distributing this publication and increasing the awareness about the dedication and efforts of the students and sponsors who have participated in the Student Employment

Program. I will ensure you receive a copy when it is completed. On behalf of the Board of Directors of the British Columbia Heritage Trust I would like to take this opportunity to wish you success in your continuing studies. I would also like to thank you for your assistance in the display of the "As Found" drawings for the final presentation. Your efforts definitely added to the success of this event.

Yours sincerely,
J. Pauline Rafferty
Program Manager
British Columbia Heritage Trust

~~~~~~~~~~~~~~~~~~~~~~~

I was happy for Lorie when she told us of her sailing experience. The great friendship she had established with her fellow students in a rather short time demonstrated how she was well liked and respected for her dedication and hard work in the school of architecture. I was relieved that she was taking a little time off from her work schedule which had followed immediately at the end of classes. She put so much of herself into everything she did so it was important that she made room for this recreation. I imagined she found the salty fragrance of the ocean breezes absolutely exhilarating. The movement of the little sailboat over the waves with lapping and splashing sounds would have relaxed her mind and body. Her artist's eye would have taken in the sights all around her. Her heart would have ached with the beauty.

During Lorie's second year at UBC she informed us that the School of Architecture would be offering studies abroad. Any student wishing to participate in these studies could only be eligible by way of maintaining good grades along with submissions of high quality work assignments.

It was obvious Lorie was determined to qualify for a spot in the group which would travel to school in Athens. I will never forget her call telling us for the first time about her plans. "Studies abroad"—just the sound of those words sent a shock wave through me. I knew Lorie was excited about the prospect of travel and all the experiences awaiting her in Europe, and I tried to sound happy for her. But my gut reaction told me something else that I could not put a name to. Having my youngest child, although grown and trying to be somewhat independent, separated from us at such a distance and for an undetermined length of time, initially overwhelmed me. This unease stayed with me for several days.

Two letters in a birthday card Lorie sent to her grandmother in October 1985:

~~~~~~~~~~~~~~~~~~~~~~~~~

Dear Grandma, I hope your eightieth was great! I wish I could have been there! You'll be hearing from me soon.

Lots of Love, Lorie

~~~~~~~~~~~~~~~~~~~~~~

I received the money you sent and two letters... thank you very much! The cost of living here is pretty high and so is school. Things are going very well for me. I'm working quite hard and seem to base everything around architecture. I do miss painting, but I have been doing a little to keep in touch. I've made a lot of friends here—nearly all in architecture or studying it. I think I made the right decision coming here. Somehow I'll be able to connect art and architecture. I was in an art show here at the Phoenix Gallery in Vancouver. It was called "Art of Architects." I had one painting and two drawings in it. I got to meet a lot of architects there. My living accommodations are terrific. I'm living with an architect who's working on Expo '86, and another student. Our place is the main floor of an old house that has been modernized. We have three bedrooms, a large bathroom, dining room, study, living room, large kitchen, attic storage, balcony, backyard garden, fireplace in the study, stained glass windows, front entrance and front porch…it's a large and happy place. We all get along very well. I am twenty min. from Univ. by bus or bike. I'm also only 1½ blocks from the water. We live in Kitsalano district.

Take care. See you at Xmas. Love, Lorie

~~~~~~~~~~~~~~~~~~~~~~~~~

It was 1985. Lorie would be home for Christmas, as would Todd and Kim. I was working full time, and trying to handle all the details that Christmas brings. I wanted everything to be perfect. Lorie's mind was not only on the holidays, but quite naturally on her upcoming travels. She had applied herself diligently, and so had won the opportunity to go to school in Athens and to travel while in Europe. She would be returning to Vancouver in a few days before flying to London, England where a Canadian journalist friend would meet her. While at home in Swift Current she ran errands, organized things to take to Greece, and visited with her friends. With everything going on, time seemed to run out before we could have a quiet hour exclusively with Lorie. Surely there were thoughts she needed to share with us, details we should have asked about, or advice we should have given. Because she would be with fellow students and with even a couple of their UBC professors, we felt that our girl would be in good company.

The question of safety never came up. How could any of us have known?

PART TWO

"I'M HAVING THE TIME OF MY LIFE!"

Lorie was to land in London early on New Year's Eve. She had purchased an outfit she thought suitable for seeing the New Year in with G., her Canadian friend. Luck was not with her, as the flight was delayed, landing mid-morning of January 1, 1986. Perhaps this was a portent of incidents to follow, but Lorie and G. celebrated the occasion in a quiet way. He was very kind, and gave Lorie a place to sleep off her jet lag. He then showed her around London, explained its transportation, and provided other useful information. For a few days they toured parts of the city with another Canadian couple. Lorie was thrilled with everything she saw. Her plans were to return to London after completing studies and travels with her UBC group. Her first visit to London was soon over, and she continued on to Athens where she met up with her classmates.

Her phone calls and letters to us were glowing; she was so very happy to have arrived in this beautiful country with its long, artistic history. Classes were inspiring; the many class tours were an education in themselves; and she was learning so much. "I'm having *the time of my life*" is how she explained her feelings to her dad and I. She also thanked us for giving her this wonderful opportunity. At that, we felt amply rewarded. Lorie's address was Clare's House, 24 Sorvoloy St. METS, Athens, Greece 11636. From there she made a habit of going for runs at Olympic Stadium, a building with a lot of marble and that offered a view of the Acropolis. Within walking distance of her hotel there was a market every Friday with cheap food including plentiful oranges and lemons. Tavernas offered bottles of retsina for forty drachmas, equal to forty Canadian cents. People tended to drink retsina instead of less pure water. Lorie and her group had to adjust to Greek business hours that were 8:00 a.m. to 2:00 p.m. Greeks usually slept from 6:00 p.m. to 10:00 p.m. at which time they would dine. Dinner was a very social time.

While touring with her group one day, Lorie became separated from it when she had become entranced with a special building she was photographing. Taking in all the wonders around them, no one in her group immediately noticed Lorie was not with them. When she became aware she was alone, she became disoriented and felt some panic. This young, tall and blond beauty had attracted the attention of Greek men in the area, and they started to approach her, making suggestive gestures. Fortunately for her, another man, a Canadian, had noted her predicament, and quickly came to her rescue. Astonishingly, this young gentleman was an architect and a Canadian diplomat. He invited Lorie to join him for a cup of coffee so she could recover while they chatted. She later told me of their conversation. She had been intrigued with his ideas of practicing architecture in needy areas of the world. He eventually saw her safely back to her group, but not before arranging to meet over a glass of orzo.

As soon as Lorie had arrived in Greece she knew she required a good quality camera to record the many sights she was privileged to tour. We complied with her wishes and sent her a Minolta. It arrived in time for her twenty-fourth birthday, and she was thrilled and grateful to have it. Even that time was not without complications. Getting the camera parcel through Greek customs presented a problem. There was a language barrier, and the clerk was not interested in being helpful. Lorie became very frustrated and was getting close to tears. Just then, a young postal employee witnessed the confusion and her distress and came to her rescue. He could speak and understand just enough English to sort out the problem, and, once more, Lorie was wonderfully relieved and grateful. In the days that followed, Lorie got to know this young man who obviously adored her natural blond beauty, true blonds being rarely seen in most parts of Greece. She was very busy with her studies and tours, but made time to enjoy an occasional cup of coffee or glass of orzo with this endearing fellow.

The following are letters to or from Lorie while she was attending school in Greece, winter of 1986.

Visiting Istanbul, Turkey for ten days with twelve classmates in March of 1986:

~~~~~~~~~~~~~~~~~~~~~~~~

… it is cold in Turkey. It is really important to travel in groups–especially women! Everyone has bought a lot of scarves and long black coats so we don't look like rip-off targets so much! The students on the trip are all terrific. Very few personal conflicts have come up which is amazing considering we all live together as well as work and socialize together. This is the best thing I could ever have done. We met a lot of really interesting people—they were mostly Muslim and their attitude towards other people (tourists) was warm and helpful. It was inspiring for a suspicious North American like me! We were taken to a lot of really interesting places with mosques and minarets all over, a water pipe and teahouse, Turkish baths, belly dancing club, rug and leather bazaars and a five hundred year old spice bazaar! We were given onsite lecture tours. Another thing I've learned is that North Americans are a lot cleaner than Greeks and Turks for sure. The hole-in-the-ground toilets are revolting (they were even on the train!).”

~~~~~~~~~~~~~~~~~~~~~~

Dear Mom and Dad,
    I've decided on an A.D.S. topic on Classical Concept of Space compared with Byzantine Concept of Space. I've done a lot of sketches and photographs. We travelled to the Island of Lesbos via rail and ferry connection. It is a perfect blend of Greek and Turkish culture. Six of us are working on two sites; one a Roman villa ruin and one a Greek house ruin with a tile mosaic floor. The concept is to design a prototype museum to be used at various archaeological sites. Our client is the Lesbos Archaeological Society who may or may not fund our projects to be built (therefore a possible job!)…

~~~~~~~~~~~~~~~~~~~~~~

Dear Mom and Dad,
    Love the island of Hydra. I feel alive! It is a fortified island with tons of mosques and churches in the hills. Lots of windmills. We have good quality meals cooked before our eyes—freshly caught octopus, squid and lots of Shellfish. No motor vehicles are allowed on the island—only donkeys! I'm looking forward to exploring more once school is done.

                        Will write again soon—Love, Lorie

~~~~~~~~~~~~~~~~~~~~~~

On April 5, 1986 Libyan agents bombed La Belle nightclub in West Berlin, killing three people and injuring two hundred twenty-nine. In retaliation, the USA bombed Libya on April 14, 1986. Because Libya is just across the Mediterranean Sea from Greece, we were once more concerned about Lorie's safety since she was visiting the Greek Isles at the time.

We heard of the Chernobyl Nuclear Power Plant disaster in Ukraine and how the fire and explosion had released large quantities of radioactive contamination into the atmosphere and how it had spread over much of Western USSR and Europe. Our first thought was of Lorie's invitation to travel to Poland to visit her classmate, Lidia, for Christmas. We were much relieved when she told us she had cancelled those plans.

Lorie received this letter from her grade six teacher:

~~~~~~~~~~~~~~~~~~~~~~~~~

Prince Albert, Sask., March 1986—Dear Lorie, How good to hear from you, and to hear about your stay in Greece! It all sounds so interesting and exciting. I am not surprised that you are doing something like this. You are one who will get the most out of life. It is hard for me to realize that it is nearly two years since I visited with you in Swift Current and you have completed one and a half years of architecture at U.B.C. I am so pleased that you were chosen for the scholarship program on a studies abroad program. Congratulations! I'm very proud of you! I am interested to hear that you plan to take a term off and work for an architect in London. You'll love London! I am going back for my eighth time this August. Good luck in all your endeavours. Enjoy your stay in Europe, but come home safely. Hope to see you sometime in the not too distant future. Thanks for taking time to write to me. I still have that piece of art you did for me in Gr. VI pinned to my bulletin board. It says, "Keep smiling—it makes people wonder what you've been up to."

Take care. Happy Easter!
Love, Phyllis MacKay.

~~~~~~~~~~~~~~~~~~~~~~~

Dear Mom and Dad, April 7, 1986—School is almost over—it's hard to finish things up because the weather is sooo beautiful. No stress here! I guess I did o.k. in my last project—my prof. is publishing a book and he's using my design as an example. He is having a model built of it—neat, eh?! I ended up liking him—I thought we wouldn't get along at all. He's trying to set me up with his son—a doctor in the Swedish army! (Who is moving to Vancouver in 4 months). I met him—he's okay. His mom is Swedish...

Love, Lorie.

~~~~~~~~~~~~~~~~~~~~~~

Swift Current, Sask.,
April 21/86

Dear Lorie,

We were very happy to hear from you and especially to get the best birthday gift Dad could have gotten; he was very pleased; I could just see him light up and it lasted all day! You sounded so good on the phone and by your letters also for which we are extremely grateful, an answer to our prayers. Now all we have to worry about is a war and your safety! We are of course concerned about your safety in Europe and hope no one mistakes you or your classmates for Americans since they seem to be fair game anywhere. We trust you will use good judgment and keep abreast of developments in any country you are in or planning to go to. Other than that all we can do is continue to pray for your health and safety. So many people ask us about you and what you're doing so after hearing about your scholarship we put a little blurb in the local paper telling of your whereabouts and your studies. Your high school art teacher said, 'That makes me feel real proud!' So take care and keep well.

All our love, from Mom and Dad.

~~~~~~~~~~~~~~~~~~~~~~~~

July 18/86—Dear Wendy, Hello Dearie! How're the wedding plans coming? I'll be in London then I imagine—until mid December. April 26 I arrived in Italy and went directly to Venice. It is the home of the great architect Palladio and his wonderful buildings are scattered all around the area. I was to meet up with classmates from Greece but instead I met a restoration artist. His family (uncle, cousins, etc.) run a restoration art company which has been in the family for three hundred years. I stayed with them for a month before I left for France. During that time we toured much of Italy—Rome, Florence, Riviera, Sienna, Milan, etc, etc. It was wonderful…a dream…

Love, Lorie

~~~~~~~~~~~~~~~~~~~~~~

After departing Greece, and while touring parts of Europe with her classmates, Lorie phoned us for money. She gave us the name of the postal location in Venice, Italy where she would await the money's arrival. She had become acquainted with an Italian family who were art restorers. This work that involved repairing very old, precious and valuable works of art pulled at her heart. She made the difficult decision to drop out of her classmates' tour so that she could immerse herself in this wonderful experience.

Another stumbling block interfered with her pleasure at being surrounded with artworks she had only dreamed of. There was a delay in the money reaching her. While waiting, she was soon completely out of resources, and relied solely on the kindness of the family of restorers she was staying with. She was totally frustrated and embarrassed to be dependent on these new friends. Her frantic phone call was upsetting for us. We were disturbed to hear her in such a state, especially since we had followed her postal instructions. I did my best to calm her while assuring her that we would look into the problem immediately. Her dad came to the rescue. He met with our bank manager that day to explain the problem. The manager assured us the needed funds would arrive within a couple of days. When Lorie received the needed funds, we all relaxed.

It was difficult for Lorie to leave Italy where she had become so attached to the kind family, and to the skills she was learning from them. It had always been her plan to find work with an architectural firm in London where she hoped to gain valuable experience before returning to UBC to complete her degree. G. and other Canadian friends in London were expecting her. As she said her farewells in Italy, she gave her heartfelt promise that she would return some day.

~~~~~~~~~~~~~~~~~~~~~~~~

London, England
June 27/86

Dear Mom and Dad, I finally have gotten my mind and pen together for a letter writing session! How are you two? I really miss you—I'd love to spend time at the lake right about now. Mom, you're most likely running yourself ragged with the Dutch Treat. Do take care not to overdo it.

My money arrived the day we had expected it to—no problem getting it either. It was enough to get me into an apt., and get a few essential things for work (pens, drafting equipment, etc.) There are a lot of times when G. has had to bail me out of financial difficulty so I owe him a lot. I'm really fortunate that he's so wonderful about it all.

My job is wonderful...I am sooo lucky to have gotten it. I'm making fifty pounds (or $15.00 per hr.) for a thirty-five hr. wk. I am constantly doing over time, but I haven't been claiming it—as it's more important to "impress" right now than to make lots of money.

I'm an architect-in-training, officially and I'm currently designing roof access to Victoria and Albert Museum - no small job! Our firm has three offices–the main one where I am has thirty-five people working there. This job was the only interview I had...I started work immediately after they interviewed me! (Within forty-eight hrs of arriving in Britain!) I have worked myself into a position with the history dept. and therefore the Victoria and Albert Museum. I've actually had meetings with the electrical engineers to discuss the placement of electrical cables and outlet boxes! My supervisors in the office are great at teaching me the ropes of English office protocol. Tony is my direct supervisor and Maggie is his supervisor. She's the only woman architect other than me and a female interior designer.

Socially life is pretty exciting. Besides G. I've met several of his friends. One guy is a journalist from Canada...Saskatchewan...Saskatoon...had been in my second year drama class...I knew him very well!! Small world. He studied journalism at U of R later and got a scholarship to work for the news agency G. works at. His mom is a published writer in Sask. G's friend John is a prof. at the London School of Economics and we go out with him and his girlfriend. Another of G's friends is a BBC cameraman (Canadian from B.C.). His girlfriend is also working here. I've met a lot of people at the office but not much socializing goes on in a big way. (I expected a lot more considering the amount of young people working there). Once we had an office party, once we had a big dinner at a restaurant for a guy who was leaving, and one wk-end there was a party in Portsmouth, a coastal town outside of London where we have an office. Also there is a Canadian UBC student working at the office—he is a yr. ahead of me. Neither of us had any idea the other was in London until I started work. Rob is a great guy and we spend a lot of time together. We held a luncheon for the office on July 1st and showed slides of Canadian Architecture. We served Canadian beer and cheddar cheese. 35 people came so it was quite a success. (But a lot of work!) The wk-end before that he and I rented a car and drove around part of England (we spent Saturday in Portsmouth at the office social). We saw Canterbury Cathedral, Brighton (Resort Town), Stonehenge and Aylesbury (similar rock formations) and Bath. The countryside is beautiful! The good thing about my job is that I get three day wk-ends which is great for touring and site seeing.

There is sooo much in London to see and do...I love it here!! G. and I and friends have gone out to a lot of theatre, both "Big name" and "Fringe" theatre. A big production we went to was "Les Miserables", a Victor Hugo play. It was a musical and was absolutely terrific! The theatre district is in Soho, the same area my office is in. My office is just off Regent St. (a famous street) and really close to major shopping strips like the well known "Seville Row" suit street and Oxford St.

I also have become friends with a girl I met in Venice...a Canadian, studied Architecture at U of Manitoba and worked for Leslie's father in Calgary last summer. She's really a sweet girl and it's great to have a "girlfriend"—really the only female friend I have here (okay by me!). The guys have their girlfriends but I haven't found any soul mates among them yet. I've had several visitors in the last while—Wendy and Greg (the girl I worked with last summer and her husband…they were both in Greece on Studies Abroad). They stayed with me for five days. Just prior to that Beth, a classmate from UBC and Studies Abroad stayed for five days.

My studio room is okay…it's starting to feel like home. My landlady is a young, black social worker with two cute nice boys and no husband. I rarely see her but she is very pleasant. I share a bathroom with them but it is fine as I am up and out early and in late at night—even on wk-ends. So, basically, that brings you up to date with what is going on with me. G. and I are seeing each other a lot, which is nice, but I would rather keep things at a less serious level. We did have a bit of a discussion when he made a down payment on an apt. close to my office for "us", but I didn't really want to do that. I'm content to stay in my little place and be somewhat independent–for at least a while. It was great to finally get organized enough to go through my papers, etc. and discover the addresses I do and do not have. I have a bit of a list for those I do need…Grandma, Todd and Kim, Elsie Wilson, Dicksons, Utigards, Grace, Dorothy, Joan, U Of B.C. Arch School, Sask. Arts Board.

I haven't really figured out my future but I haven't needed to either. I could stay forever if I sold my ticket but then, on the other hand, I'm already feeling guilty for not going back to school this fall! I think the happy medium, or my original plan of returning at Xmas will be the best (or stay here until Dec. 31 and you two could visit me! You would love it here!) Think about that one—time will tell as to my plans.

That just about brings you up to date on my British existence. I have a book to write about Italy, and France with G. Italy was the magical time because I was totally submerged into the Italian way of life in Venice. The man I met there was a restoration artist with his family (old family business). I really liked him a lot even though he hardly spoke English!! (or rather, he didn't like to). His best friend, an English prof. at the University of Venice offered to give me free Italian lessons!! I would love to go back (and I might).

I feel badly that I haven't been in contact more often with you or anyone but there is so much happening in my life (and has been for so long). I'm having nothing but success with my camera! It takes wonderful pictures! I used it for work once to photograph items for my design project at the VandA Museum and it worked well. (My boss liked it). I must go...I have a lot to do today and it seems I never get time alone (G. is at Oxford today interviewing someone).

Take care and write soon. Love, Lorie

~~~~~~~~~~~~~~~~~~~~~~~

London, England
July 15/86

Dear Marnie—Hi there! I'm alive and well and living in London. After classes I headed for the Greek islands with five other classmates. It was a great time. We got to Syros, Tinos, Mykonos, Delos and Santorini. It was during the time the states bombed Libia so travelling and being sooo close to the trouble got a bit scary. I headed straight for Venice when I got to Italy. I had such incredible luck there...I met a restoration architect whose family had a large, old firm in Venice (Giovani—yet another nice guy!) I stayed for six weeks and did some drawings for him on a restoration job of a palace on the Grand Canal. His uncle was a great guy to work for but his English was limited (and so is my Italian!) Giovanni was good about translating, but it was difficult. I did learn a lot from them and sometimes I regret having left.

This past wk-end my Dutch cousin and his wife and son took me sailing, embarking at Brighton. They sailed here from Holland last wk. My dad's first cousin is a naval architect so we had a lot to chat about. They are taking G. and I out this wkend too.

I met G. in Paris after a tour of the rest of Italy (yes, it was difficult leaving!). He had just returned from India. I hadn`t seen him since New Yr`s day. Anyway I swiftly fell in love (again!) and we spent two fabulous wks. on the Riviera (Cannes, Nice, Monocco, Lyon). We caught the last part of the Cannes festival, sun tanned on gorgeous beaches, drank pernod at street cafes and explored a lot of mountain villages. There were of course the art galleries filled with Matisse and Piccassos. Yes, I was in heaven! We spent five days in Paris, afterward. We stayed in Montmartre, an area known for its artists and cafes. (I saw every possible thing I could in five days—a lot of running.)

The day we got to London G. took me to a Laurie Anderson concert—it was soooo terrific! My place is a studio apt.—small and expensive, but that`s standard for London...

Love, Lorie

~~~~~~~~~~~~~~~~~~~~~~~

Lorie had started a letter to us three times during July 25 and 27, 1986:

> Friday, July 25—Dear Mom and Dad, Here I am held up in a laundrette waiting for two wks of laundry to be renewed! What a way to spend a sunny afternoon (sun is rare in this country!) I am enjoying this place and my job and my pay cheque a lot! It`s a whole new concept, this working business. I'm always busy and under-the-gun at work and socially. It's a rare occasion I get to see the neighbourhood where I 'live', so today is quite interesting. Did I mention that I live in a Black Baptist neighbourhood! It`s a pretty neat place and I am used to being the minority after Greece and Italy. (I think there are only ten white people on my block!) So much for racist statements, eh! My studio room is working out fine…

~~~~~~~~~~~~~~~~~~~~~~~

> Friday July 25—Dear Mom and Dad, I knew that writing a letter home would make me homesick and sure enough the last letter I wrote did just that! Also the presentation I gave on Canada July 1 added to the fact. Our office is going through a lot of staff changes, so work is missing the element of familiarity sometimes…

~~~~~~~~~~~~~~~~~~~~~~~

> Sunday July 27th—Dear Mom and Dad—I hopefully can catch a few minutes of time to write a note. I spend a lot of time on trains…

~~~~~~~~~~~~~~~~~~~~~~~

A letter I sent to Lorie on August 8, 1986 was returned to me unopened some weeks later. This was coincidentally the day of her death.

Dear Lorie, Got an unexpected pleasant surprise when I was able to get home for four days—first time since April. Kim and Todd came north and convinced me to take the opportunity to come back with Todd—Kim is running the show for me working and Dad picked me up there. It`s been great being back and not have to be on duty all day every day—Dad and I have really missed one another. I got my hair cut, had a doctor's appointment and had a dental check, have seen most of our friends and so on. The city looks so nice with the downtown improvements—lovely flower planters, etc. Todd comes back tonight and we leave in a.m. for the north. Dad is coming up for our anniversary, and then I have twelve days alone (no students) until he comes for the long wk-end in September. He'll stay a week then when we'll put the golf course to bed for the winter, also cottage. Thought you'd enjoy the enclosed. Hope to hear from you soon. Everyone who hears about your job and opportunity thinks you`re so lucky. All for now.

Love, Mom and Dad

~~~~~~~~~~~~~~~~~~~~~~~~~

Jack and I were so pleased for Lorie and the way her plans were working out. We knew she was thrilled to be working on the Victoria-Albert Museum especially since it is the world's greatest museum of art and design. Her assignment involved photographing and drawing the roof structure of the VandA Museum that would be undergoing structural changes. Immersed in her work there she would lose track of time that sometimes made her very late for dates with G. and their friends. G. knew how dedicated she was and how much she wished to impress her employers. Because London is such a huge metropolis, and because he would be showing Lorie around, G. thought it would be more convenient if she stayed with him. Later, when Lorie told us of his kind offer, she explained to me, "At that point, I just wanted a little place of my own."

Since Lorie was twenty-four, it was her decision to make, but I was secretly proud of her choice. I thought to myself, *Well, I guess I brought her up right.*

There came a time when her dad and I wished that she had been living with someone. But, how could any of us have predicted that.

We were so pleased when our Dutch cousins met Lorie on July 11, 1986 at Brighton, where they were docked. Jack and I had enjoyed our weekend sail with them on the North Sea during our visit three years before. It was special meeting Jack's first cousin, Adrie Ivens and his wife, Bea who lived in Graauw, Netherlands. Their son, Manfred had visited us in Swift Current before Todd and his friends took him on a white water rafting experience. Some years later Manfred and his fiance, Yolanda had also travelled to stay with us at our cottage. Lorie was thrilled having her first yachting experience on a weekend sail along England's coastline. We knew Bea and Adrie, along with Manfred and a friend had met her on July 18 in the harbour of Yarmouth on the Isle of Wight for a second sail. The first afternoon they took her by bus to Alum Bay, near Needles to see the coloured rocks. They descended to the beach by chair lift. That evening Manfred, his friend, and Lorie took their rowing dinghy to the local pub where they chatted with some locals. The next two days, very nice and sunny, were lazy times as they sailed to the east of Wight. The cousins and Lorie talked a lot, exchanging views, about student life in Canada and in the Netherlands, and about Lorie's travels through Europe. They also tried to teach Lorie some Dutch words. The cousins remember how very enthusiastic Lorie was and how great it was to have her on board. Bea and Adrie had invited her to visit them in Holland before she returned to Canada. Lorie could not have been happier. On Sunday evening they sailed to the harbour of Portsmouth and the next morning the young cousins went to London by train. They said their goodbyes at Victoria station–that was the last time they saw Lorie.

Meanwhile, Jack and I had made plans of our own. With Todd married and about to begin a second university degree, and with Lorie well on her scholastic way, following her life's desires, we had recently acted on our retirement plans. We had a contractor build a summer business which we started operating in May of 1986. The business was located in the park where we had built our cottage. At first, I handled the operation with student employees. Jack joined me during his annual holiday; he had not decided on the exact date for his own retirement. It meant a lot of responsibility and work for me in the short term, while Jack did a lot of travelling to and from this new business. In early August, Todd and Kim were able to join us at the cottage and help out. The plans were for Kim to stay to look after things while I drove back home to Swift Current with Jack and Todd, as Todd was to have an interview there with a dentist before he started his own dentistry classes. They all thought it would give me a nice break after being away from home all spring and summer. This was the first time the three of us had been together at home in some years. I was very grateful for Kim's generosity in giving me this opportunity. Just how grateful I would eventually be, and how necessary these arrangements had been, I was soon to learn.

Unknowingly, we would all be involved in an international drama before the night was over. However, while Todd went to his interview, Jack and I treated ourselves to a relaxing meal out. We went to our favourite pizza place where we enjoyed cold glasses of beer with our delicious meal. We had time to catch up on business and personal news. We revelled in the pleasure of seeing how our plans were all coming together. We had raised two children successfully, had steered them into seeking academics where both were doing well in their chosen fields. We would both soon be retired, and we had a relaxing, seasonal business to ease us away from full-time careers in police work and nursing. We had worked hard and planned well. Now we were beginning to reap our rewards, just like it should be. At least, that's what we thought, what we believed. It had been a simple, but wonderful evening when we had looked back, and ahead as we enjoyed the present.

Back at the house, we met Todd and heard about his interview, and of his plans. We were just having a quiet, relaxing family time together. We would soon head for bed and a much needed good night's sleep. The next memories are fixed in my being and will forever be a part of my soul. The television was still on when I went to the bathroom to prepare for bed. Todd and his dad were about to turn in. The bathroom of our en suite had a small window looking onto the driveway. It was partly open to let in some cool evening air. I heard a vehicle door closing nearby, and then, a second later, another car door. My ears did not perk up until I knew someone was walking along our driveway. Who could that be? I thought. It's a bit late for anyone to stop by, especially without phoning first. Then I looked out the window, and I drew in a quick breath. Two RCMP officers in uniform. Policemen never come to the house. They phone, on occasion, to give Jack, their senior officer, information or to ask advice. My mind was suddenly on high alert—I felt a shock wave enter my body. The doorbell rang. I heard voices. Jack called me.

Newborn Lorie Gaye at
Spalding Hospital, Feb. 1962

With Mom at Onion Lake

With Kip at Onion Lake

With Mom at Onion Lake

With Chris at Goodsoil 1965

With Chris at Banff 1964

Lorie's note to Mom at Moosomin 1968

Family vacation

After accident at Madge Lake 1970

With Trudy 1972

Flying with her dad in 1972

Brave in body brace 1978

With Phyllis McKay

Friends with graduation awards

Graduation at Swift Current 1980

High school graduation 1980

At family cottage

Christmas at cottage

Bridesmaid for Dot

At Emma Lake Art
School – Acrylic

In Red Cross Car 1984

Studying in Vancouver 1985

Surrounded by her art work

B.C. Architecture School jacket - Athens, Greece

Sailing with friends 1985

Stamps from
England and Greece

Architecture firm – London,
England

Cousin Adrie's sailboat 1986

Lee-Knight family cottage

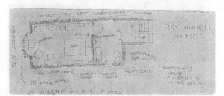

Bedsit – London, England

House where bedsit located

Meadow Lake Provincial Park – charcoal

Trees in relief – oil

Theme for grad 1978 – pastel

Park scene – charcoal

Commissioned work – oil

Blue jays – pastel

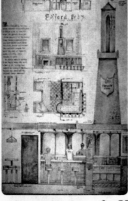

Drawing assignment for UBC
School of Architecture

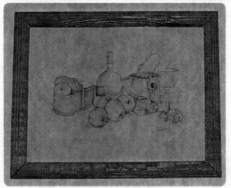

Still life – pointillism

LORIE G. LEE-KNIGHT

A rose herself,
Alas, she has lived,
No longer than the rose:
One morning, her glory.

Malherbe

Lorie promised to be a brilliant architect, and a great artist. The fact that, although Lorie left only a small body of largely "student work", the localized beginnings of such a creative process had been firmly established when her life was tragically cut short. Her mother, Mrs. Ruth Lee-Knight, in a letter to Lorie's former teacher, Mrs. Phyl MacKay, of Prince Albert, talks candidly about Lorie's early life in Prince Albert.

"Close to her heart were memories of her 6th grade at John Diefenbaker School. She was fortunate to have Mrs. Phyllis MacKay as her teacher, friend, and guide. This special person recognized the budding talent and sensitivities in Lorie. They remained friends and corresponded until Lorie's untimely death. She greatly admired her teacher to whom she was always grateful."

Following is Lorie's philosopy as interpreted by her mother:

Lorie's philosophy - Life is wonderful, difficult and short

There is so much to see, beauty everywhere, we need only open our eyes to appreciate it.

Many barriers are put in our way so we must struggle continually to overcome those we can and cope with those we can't.

There is never enough time to experience everything, travel to all the places, see all the sights, meet all the people and accomplish all the goals. Therefore, we must not be bound by ceremony and insignificant detail but must surely get on with those things that are important.

Writings collected by Mrs. Phyllis McKay

Drawing of Victoria and Albert Museum
roof top – London, England

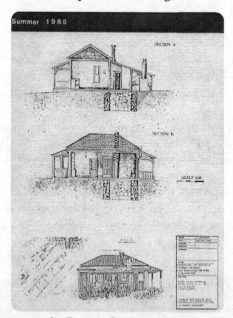

Drawings for British Columbia Heritage Trust

PART THREE

THE DREAM ENDS

*L*orie had every Friday off and she had spent the morning of that Friday organizing her bedsit. She had art supplies in one corner, text books on a shelf, cosmetics and hair supplies on the bureau. Several photos of family members and friends were tucked in around the mirror. There was a hot plate, an electric kettle, and a small refrigerator on a cupboard with canned goods on the shelving below. A bowl on the small table held fresh fruit. There were two wooden chairs to match the table. The single bed, night stand and upholstered chair completed her room. A closet held her wardrobe and luggage. A window looked out at the trees and flowers in the back garden below. The bathroom was just outside her bed-sit. Three other young women, all out at that time, occupied other rooms on the second floor level. The owner of the building who lived on the main floor with her two young boys was a social worker, and she was away on vacation that week. Before leaving she had turned off the only phone in the house.

Satisfied that her little home away from home was in order, Lorie went out for her daily jog. She loved seeing the English style homes, so different from those in Canada. There were trees everywhere, and hedges, with ivy crawling across the brickwork of most homes. She could often catch sight of flowers among the greenery. She probably thought of her grandmother who had been born in England, and who had a lifelong love of flowers. She likely intended to include descriptions of the green and blooming sights in her next letter to Grandma, and to Mom who had inherited a love of all growing things. She headed for the nearby park where she liked to run a circuit, usually for twenty to thirty minutes, depending on the weather. Back at the house Lorie unlocked the door. Panting from her exertion she let the heavy door slam shut behind her. It should have locked automatically. But did it? Running up the stairs Lorie was likely looking forward to her shower after which she would dress for the stage play. G. had planned to meet her at the train station nearest the theatre. She had written glowing letters home about theatre performances they had been to, and told of others they planned for. London was so exciting!

****

When Lorie did not arrive for their planned date that August day in 1986, G. was not too concerned. She had probably gone back to the office to complete some work before joining him he thought. He knew time often got away on her. He waited. A few hours later as G. disconsolately walked alone along the crowded street away from the theatre he suddenly heard Lorie call out his name. She sounded frightened, and he was immediately alerted. At the sound of her voice he felt the hair stand up on the back of his neck. He stopped to look around, up and down the street. He did not understand what was happening. There was no sign of her anywhere. Later, at home, he was restless, finding it difficult to get to sleep.

****

During the night there was a loud knock on his apartment door. When he went to the door he was surprised to find two London policemen there. He answered, that yes, he was indeed G., a journalist currently working in London, but from British Columbia, Canada. Yes, he knew Lorie Gaye Lee-Knight, a Canadian girl he was dating; no, he had not seen her last evening as she had failed to meet for their theatre date. The officers were telling him something, but he could not comprehend *what they said. Found dead in the bathroom off her bedsit? Lorie—vivacious, beautiful Lorie? The girl with the golden hair, deep-blue eyes, and the infectious, bubbly laugh. His Lorie? His name and address were found in her effects. Would he please come with them to identify the body. Shaken and gripping the door frame, G. almost collapsed before the officers guided him to the nearest chair. He held his head in his hands. How could this be? A moan escaped him before he nodded. He wanted to phone another Canadian journalist to accompany them if that would be all right. They agreed, and Scott, incredulous, soon arrived.*

Dumbfounded, I left the bedroom, and from the hallway I saw Jack standing with the two RCMP officers. He was leaning over and gripping the kitchen counter as the men spoke quietly. What was this about? Why did Jack want me? He was telling me something, but it did not register with me. *What? Lorie? Why? Where? There's got to be a mistake, not Lorie. There are other girls living in that house, it has got to be one of them.* It couldn't be Lorie, she's only been living in London for five or six weeks. Jack's arm was now around me, and Todd had somehow joined us. The policemen were quietly speaking…a known sex offender…he had broken parole by leaving his home country of Ireland. He had been in England for only a matter of hours, apparently looking for his next victim. He should not have gained entry into another country. What did Ireland, courts, judges have to do with our girl? My mind ceased to function, and I wanted to vomit. We, Lorie's dad and mom and brother, held on to one another and cried the first rivers of tears that were to flow in the years that followed.

****

The next few days were a blur, but soon we were all on a plane flying for England. G. and Scott met us at Heathrow. They took Todd home to G.'s place. Jack and I found ourselves in the London apartment of Inspector Del Klatt, a Foreign Service Officer with the RCMP. This was to be our headquarters during our stay in London. London, where we would view our beautiful girl. Where we would travel to Scotland Yard to meet the team assigned to this case, where they would explain evidence that helped them solve this crime. Where we would meet the owner of the architectural firm that Lorie had worked with. Where we would inexplicably run into Lorie's grade six teacher, Phyllis MacKay, on a London street, and where we explained to her why we were there. London, a city of Lorie's dreams where her career was just beginning, where she had just begun to spread her wings, for the first time, independent of her family, earning a salary, living in quarters of her own choosing, a fledgling.

The news media was merciless. From the first day calls came regularly with such foolish questions. What did we think of London? As if that mattered. News of "the Mountie's girl" along with her photo appeared in every newspaper and on television newscasts. *This Mountie had given years of dedicated service to the Force in Canada, maintaining law and order and aiding any individuals in need, but his girl was not afforded the same protection in another country. Her mother had given many years to the profession of nursing, doing her best to alleviate the suffering of others. But, her daughter had not been spared. Both her parents had sacrificed so Lorie and her brother could have the advantage of a good education. What sense could they make of any of that, and where was the mercy?*

****

Back home we found ourselves trying to make plans for a memorial service. Lorie's body would not be released until

Scotland Yard and the courts had completed their work. Jack and I felt we needed to have our friend, the Reverend Ivor Ottrey, conduct the service since he was the clergyman who had been a part of Lorie's life. We never forgot Lorie's recognition of an aura around Ivor's head. He no longer lived in Swift Current but had moved with his family to Medicine Hat, Alberta. We phoned. He came. He brought his younger son, by then confined to a wheelchair. They had lost their first son to the cruel muscular degeneration. Lorie's friends attended the service in a group and took part in the service. After her big brother, Todd, read G's touching eulogy, Rev. Ottrey gave his own personal heartfelt message. Ivor's address began with, "Why should so terrible a thing happen to an honest, upright, godly woman? Like a stone dropped in water, ripples will reach far beyond. So our actions whether good or bad will affect many others; kindness travels and unfortunately so does evil, and many, as we know choose evil; hence the tragedy we face today…"

PART FOUR

LETTERS

Before her death Lorie received this letter from a classmate:

> "...I've gained a tremendous amount of respect for you. You have a quality that very few people do—an open mind and a willingness to learn, not just about architecture but about everything...You seem to recognize that there is a place to strive to and that you work very hard at learning and growing and listening to others. That's a rare and admirable quality. I think you're a really good person, Lorie—you've certainly taught me something and I'm glad I spent a few months in Greece with you."

~~~~~~~~~~~~~~~~~~~~~~~

From Ed Lysyk, Director of Corporate Security, Wardair International. Before Ed retired from the RCMP he had been Jack's officer commanding.

> Dear Jack:
> A week ago while flying to Toronto I read of the horrible event experienced by your family. I tried to get a message to you that I would arrange any flight you might need to London (gratis) and in that I go to London frequently, I would do anything I could for you at that end. I later heard you were already there. The other thing I wanted to do was send along my sincere sympathy to Ruth and yourself. We, being fortunate, of course have no idea of how traumatic an experience like that can be–it has to be terrible. Jack, if there still remains anyway I can help

out, please do let me know. In the meantime we do often think of your terrible experience and do in a small way share your grief".

Sincerely yours, Ed Lysyk

~~~~~~~~~~~~~~~~~~~~~~~~~

From Lorie's Swift Current friends:

When people were around her, they seemed to absorb her uplifting spirit. Her visions and work send forth a ripple of life transforming into a current of energy. I dreamed about Lorie about a month after she passed away.

I saw her by our bedroom door, inside our bedroom. In my dream I was sleeping and was awakened when Lorie walked into the room. I can't remember if we actually ex-changed any words but we somehow just communicated by seeing each other. I knew that she wanted to talk to Grace. All I thought about then was just the fact that I knew Grace wasn't quite ready to see her, so I made Lorie understand that. The next thing that I remembered was waking up and looking at the bedroom door, wondering if it was a dream because it did seem very real. We dreamt a lot about her around that time. We miss her a lot and are glad that she gave us her work for us to remember her by…

~~~~~~~~~~~~~~~~~~~~~~~~~

Lorie gave so generously of her time and herself to our children as a babysitter, swimming teacher and friend - we all thought she was terrific. Lorie was a lovely, talented, happy young lady who touched all who knew her…".

~~~~~~~~~~~~~~~~~~~~~~~~~

Our family wishes to express our deep sympathy to you. Lorie babysat our children when she was in high school. We saw a lot of her the summers she was a lifeguard at Cypress Park and taught swimming lessons. Michael, our oldest son, particularly, spent a good deal of time with her the summer he took bronze medal instruction. Lorie gave so generously of her time and herself to our children as a babysitter, teacher and friend—we all thought she was terrific. Lorie was a lovely, talented, happy young lady who touched all who knew her. Our hearts go out to you and your family at such a tragic loss".

~~~~~~~~~~~~~~~~~~~~~~

From our Swift Current next door neighbours:

Dear Jack and Ruth:

There are no words to express our deepest sympathy. I have cried with you and for ourselves as we too feel this loss—you were next door neighbours so many years. The Lord has allowed much pain in your lives—but, with the pain He has promised 'strength for the day'. I trust this little 'letter', as if it was from Lorie as I see and remember her, will be a comfort to you as I know she would wish it. Our sympathies to Todd and Kim too—we care and will continue to pray in the coming days.

Love, Agatha and Jake

~~~~~~~~~~~~~~~~~~~~~~

Dear Mom and Dad—Don't weep for me—I am at rest now. You both, together with God, gave me a full, happy, rewarding life—you cared, you loved always, you encouraged and nurtured me through my growing up years, recognized my talents, gave me the opportunities to develop them so that many others could enjoy the work of my hands. Just a few years ago some caring young people shared with me about God's love for me—at this time His Son gave me a New Life, a new Hope and reason for living. Again, you, Mom, helped me to grow in this New Life, rejoicing with me. Now, I count it a privilege that the Lord saw fit for me to have shared in His sufferings on my behalf. For He, too was wounded, His side was pierced–like Him, I too want to say as He did just before He died–'Father forgive them, for they know not what they do'.

I am at peace. Love, Lorie

~~~~~~~~~~~~~~~~~~~~~~~

From U of S fellow students:

Lorie was like the wind. She was always on the go, breezing in and out of people's lives which will never be the same. Occasionally she was a hurricane as she was so alive, involved and very busy. I often wondered where this energy came from? Lorie discovered a gentle breeze and it was within this breeze that she drew the spark, the foundation for everything she did. There were many special times when she would return to this breeze and rediscover her God. A time of peace and love that she would swirl into a wind as to share it with others... I remember one day she shrieked for me to witness what her father had brought her. "Look what Dad brought for me" and by those words and the way she said them I realized it wasn't the coat that she was so proud of as much as how proud she was of her dad and how he cared for her...realized she was still happy to be Daddy's little girl...it was beautiful. Robb

~~~~~~~~~~~~~~~~~~~~~~~

I haven't had a friend die before. It's only relatives who are old or sick who are supposed to die. Even when we were living together Lorie was always challenging me with things, making me do some serious soul searching and her death is no exception. This past while has made me realize what a big influence she has had on my life. As I grieve for Lorie I realize that even though her life was all too short it was very full. I was always amazed at how much she could fit into one day. Lorie set her goals high and she always managed to reach them. I know though, that even in her busy schedule and determination to be independent, her family meant a great deal to her and she loved you very much. It is for you, Lorie's family, that my most heartfelt sympathy goes out. I have come to realize that Lorie has found peace and is not suffering, but it is those left behind who must struggle with a deep hurt and loss. I know nothing I can say will take away those feelings, but I hope that there is reassurance in the fact that you are in many people's thoughts and prayers, and that this will help give you strength. There were many times when I relied on Lorie's strength and I am very proud to have had her as a friend. We are very fortunate to have someone like her touch our lives; she will always be with us in our hearts and memories. God bless you all.

~~~~~~~~~~~~~~~~~~~~~~~~

Hello. I can't tell you how many times I've started to write this letter. Your note helped me to try to put my thoughts and feelings in order. I guess I'm still disbelieving and in shock—when I heard the news I was expecting a letter from Lorie and I kept seeing her in front of me just as she was when we last met and I think of her often. I'm sorry that I was not able to attend the memorial service. However I did meet with friends (who knew Lorie too). Sometimes, we tend to think better of a person when they are gone, but in Lorie's case it would be very hard to have topped who she was while she was with us. All that you as her mother feel to be true—was true about Lorie. Though we were never constantly together, as friends sometimes are, I felt a sort of closeness with Lorie because she was loveable and real, not self-involved the way some artists can be. We met in 1983 at the U of S—I had just returned from Vancouver and Lorie was in my drawing class with Bob Christie. We worked in the studio, shared criticisms, ideas and lots of small talk about life mostly. Lorie felt like a little sister to me (as she was seven years my junior) and I shared many of my experiences about my travels and life in Vancouver. We used to joke about her going to architecture school. She would say, "I'm young, it's only three years, after I graduate I'll be able to support my expensive habit of painting!" When it came time to graduate and mount her exhibition she asked me to help her find something wild and dazzling to wear so instead of going shopping I made her a top of electric blue suede which she wore like nobody else could have (do you remember?). She came up to the painting studio to show me before her opening and I thought she looked great! But I also thought, "I hope your mother isn't too shocked!" She was so much the girl/woman still very attractive when all dressed up (older looking), but most of the time in track pants and runners so natural to Lorie's personality to be able to be herself in many situations. I was so hoping that Lorie could meet my new son, Oliver, this fall and now that I know she won't be coming I look at Oliver and really see how much I love him and give him the hug I know Lorie would have given him. Oh, God, I hope Lorie did not suffer too much pain before she died. My dreams sometimes are horrible recreations of it and sometimes I am the avenger and wake up feeling horrible and saddened to face this world in which we live! Women are so often the victim, and the men who go to prison never seem to get the help they really need. There are many women's groups in Canada trying desperately to get these laws changed. I have written letters along with others lobbying in Ottawa and I hope you could see how much your letter might help save someone's daughter in the future. These kinds of people either should be locked away for life or they should undergo therapy and be on probation for life. In a way we are all victims of the society in which we live—unless we try to change it. I hope this letter has helped. Maybe some day we will meet. I was happy to read that Todd has married (he probably doesn't remember meeting me) and hope that they can help ease your pain by giving you many grandchildren to fill the emptiness. Oliver is a joy to all of us and a constant source of growth, change and hope for our future.

~~~~~~~~~~~~~~~~~~~~~~~

During the years Lorie spent working as a lifeguard in Gull Lake, and attending the University of Saskatchewan, I had the rare opportunity to know a very wonderful and special person. Without a doubt, you know and remember all the wonderful qualities which made Lorie a favourite with all who met her—all I could possibly add to this is that she had the remarkable ability to brighten up any room simply by walking into it. She had an optimism, a manner, and particularly a laugh that was utterly contagious. I wish that her artistic ability was contagious as well—I remember seeing an exhibition of her work at the Art Gallery in Swift Current while I was working for CJFB-TV in January of 1983, and being duly impressed. When I heard the news of Lorie's death on the radio, I was preparing for a play I perform for Parks Canada at Rocky Mountain House , a National Historic Park. The play, a half-hour monologue I researched and wrote this past winter, chronicles the emotions felt by a senior clerk of the Hudson's Bay Company in 1836 after hearing of the death of his Indian wife. My first response after hearing the news was to cancel the performance, but it soon became obvious that what I was feeling was much the same as my character. The show went on that day, bearing a dedication to the memory of a very special woman named Lorie Lee-Knight...as it has in every performance since. We are hoping to expand and film the show for instructional purposes this winter—and if the "dream" comes true, I can guarantee it will bear another dedication to Lorie. My family who live in Gull Lake had the honour of knowing Lorie as well, and all of them grew to admire her as I did. We all send our best wishes to your family, and our assurances that we will never forget all the beautiful things about Lorie.

~~~~~~~~~~~~~~~~~~~~~~~~~

Lorie's former colleagues at the University of Saskatchewan were all shocked and greatly saddened to hear of her untimely death. She was a very inspiring student to work with because of her enthusiasm and dedication. Because of this, we felt that it would be appropriate to establish an award in her name at the university, to be given annually to a student displaying excellence in the visual arts. In this way, she would always be remembered at the university, and serious students would be encouraged and supported, a practice which I believe Lorie would have wholeheartedly supported. Before we begin the process of establishing this award, however, I would like to receive your approval. If there is any reason why you would prefer that we do not proceed, or if you have any input that you would like us to consider, please let me know. I await your comments before we proceed on this project. Again, I would like to extend the greatest sympathies from myself and all of Lorie's classmates at the University of Saskatchewan.

~~~~~~~~~~~~~~~~~~~~~~~~

It took me a while to get your address, or I would have written to you sooner to express my great sympathy for you over Lorie's death. I would like to let you know about the way that Lorie stood out as a quite exceptionally lovely person among the students in the Art Department here. I met her when we were both studying Medieval Art History in 1983. I was an MFA graduate student and more than twice her age and yet she responded to everyone with such genuine interest—and had such a good sense of humour—that age barriers did not exist. We all used to meet in the coffee room and Lorie was always at the centre of discussion or laughter. I do hope that by writing to you it does not make this painful tragedy worse for you. But rather that it might help you if you knew that in the most natural way Lorie has probably left a mark and brought happy shared moments to a much greater extent than many others do in a long life time. You must be wonderful parents to have had a daughter like her. Everyone one talks to shared my high opinion of her and finds the shock hard to express.

~~~~~~~~~~~~~~~~~~~~~~~~~

From Lorie's roommate's mother:

Lorie is part of our treasured garden of friendships. Lauren often spoke of their late night conversations and the bonding of their spirits...Lorie challenged every day with spirit and enthusiasm. She made every minute count... Lorie had those support facts of love and faith given by her family and friends...She never got old, was always physically active, and she never had to suffer the pain of continuous rejection... Thank you for giving her the freedom to fly with her goals and for allowing her to explore all of life.

~~~~~~~~~~~~~~~~~~~~~~~

Letters from UBC students:

My name is Lidia. I am Lorie's friend. I received letters from our friends in UBC telling me about what happened to Lorie. It is hard to comprehend how and why such unjust things happen. Lorie was a very kind person, always doing her best, both in school and as a friend. She once told me that it was you, her parents, who told her always to try to be best. She was very proud of you and her brother. I don't know if she ever told you about me. I came to Vancouver for one year to study architecture and to stay with my parents. My parents came to our studio a few times, and they always admired Lorie for how hard she worked, and how good she always looked. Lorie wrote me from Greece about her plans for holidays in Europe and for work in London. I invited her to Poland for Christmas, and I was waiting for her answer. And then I got the letters from UBC. I am sorry I won't see her any more, or see how she was just beginning to live.

~~~~~~~~~~~~~~~~~~~~~~~~~~

Lorie used to tell me about a higher level of a human being. These people possessed certain qualities which seemed to distinctly rise above the average qualities inherent in people.

She mentioned often that she had met several, and of course, there would be others. These people believed in 'a guardian angel' which would watch over the person and guide them through life. I always considered Lorie to have an angel perched on her shoulder.

~~~~~~~~~~~~~~~~~~~~~~~~

A group of us is assembling a special album to send you later this fall. I hope it will give you a better picture of Lorie's life in architecture: at UBC, in Greece and in London. Although I was ahead of Lorie in school I got to know her during the spring of her first year. We shared a tutorial and travelled to San Francisco together. Her warmth and sensitivity allowed our friendship to grow quickly. She was a talented artist and taught me a great deal. Her beautiful spirit soared and spoke unwittingly of fine parents and a solid family life. I would like to offer my condolences at this sad time.

~~~~~~~~~~~~~~~~~~~~~~~~

Through the grief, I feel, however, that Lorie's spirit still soars. The love she shared with us shall live on in our memories and give us strength.

…As both a classmate and roommate (in Athens) of Lorie's, I would like to extend to you my deepest sympathy. I know that Lorie was at an age where she was still trying to become 'independent' from family, and to 'make it on her own', yet at the same time she often spoke of you. She was so happy when you asked her to design a business building; the whole school knew that Lorie, sitting there surrounded by piles of drawings, was working on plans for her father. She was very, very, proud. One evening in our room in Athens she surprised me by pulling out a stack of family photographs, yellow with age. There was one of the two of you, dressed up for some 1960's ball, and there were Lorie and Todd, doing whatever small kids do in photographs. There was a whole stack of these pictures, and Lorie treated me to a long description of every single one. Then, when a friend came to visit us in our room, the entire show was repeated for his benefit. I know that these are small things which others may have forgotten, but in thinking of you now they came to mind, and I thought that perhaps they might be a small source of comfort.

~~~~~~~~~~~~~~~~~~~~~~~~

England! Travel! She was so excited, so bubbly, so darned insistent about it!...not a desire, but a demand. She just had to do it or she would be missing a fragment of life. Just being around Lorie and her dreams somehow kept me both amused and aware that such a joy for simply being alive on planet Earth was probably one of the greatest and richest assets any one person could have for themselves, let alone share with others and infect others as Lorie did... Finally, sweet Lorie leaves me with more than just a memory. Joy in duress is an idea that keeps her in my mind daily. She taught good lessons!

~~~~~~~~~~~~~~~~~~~~~~~~

...I was very glad that we had a chance to visit. I really appreciate your hospitality and the chance to share 'your' Lorie and 'my' Lorie. After seeing her home and town, as well as her work and hearing about her from those who knew her so well I feel I really have a good sense of just what Lorie was and what she meant to me. Just talking to you both really helped bring so much out of me and clarify just what and how I've been feeling. For me Lorie and all she brought into my life was and always will be an inspiration. I thank you for bringing her into this world!

~~~~~~~~~~~~~~~~~~~~~~~

Letters from UBC professors:

".... You should know that she will be remembered for her warm and open personality, her very real talents and her determined quest for knowledge, her sense of fun, and her many contributions to the community that is this School. Certainly she will be missed... .

Douglas Shadbolt, Director

~~~~~~~~~~~~~~~~~~~~

Lorie was a joy to all and a pleasure to work with. I got to know her better in Greece, and I can assure you that her stay there was a very happy and productive one. She enjoyed her work and her grades were at the very top of the class. Above all, however, I shall remember her not only as a student but as one of the most lovely people that I have ever met.

Yours truly, John Gaitanakis, Assistant Professor

~~~~~~~~~~~~~~~~~~~~

I got to know Lorie best last January when I spent several weeks with the UBC program in Athens. I was working with her on some of her projects and came to realize what a sweet and life-inspiring person she was... .

Sincerely yours,
Abraham Rogatnick,
Professor Emeritus, UBC

~~~~~~~~~~~~~~~~~~~~~~~

...I was a member of the staff of the School of Architecture during the Studies Abroad Program in Athens this year. I lived in Clare's House and saw the students almost every day. I knew Lorie better than I knew some of the students because of an incident which happened on New Year's Eve in London. I managed to fall and land on my face on the wet pavement, and Lorie was there in a moment with quick and efficient first aid and support. We laughed later about my arrival in Athens with a black eye, but I was grateful for her quick attention. I think this was typical of Lorie's reactions. I will remember her with affection and delight. Lorie entered into the program with enthusiasm and contributed significantly to the success of the difficult task presented to the group. She grew in confidence in her work and I believe in herself as a maturing student of architecture. I took this picture of Lorie the day in January, shortly after our arrival, when we were invited to visit the Academy. It is not open to the public, but we were taken on an extensive tour of this remarkable building by one of the Academicians and were introduced to the chairman. This was a rich and unique experience. For me, and for all of us. Lorie will always be part of our life-long memories of Athens.

<div style="text-align: right">

God bless you, Helen Jones

</div>

~~~~~~~~~~~~~~~~~~~~~~~

From a neighbour in Vancouver:

...To know Lorie was to love her. She was one of the most wonderful people whom I've ever met... Lorie brought a fresh joy, beauty, delight and laughter to the whole house...we used to marvel at her energy, her imagination, her talent, her blond loveliness but also at her diligence, intelligence and her desire to succeed...I was so glad for her courage and determination to study and travel. She was a truly splendid human being whom I shall remember with the very, very deepest warmth and love...

~~~~~~~~~~~~~~~~~~~~~~

Letters from Lorie's London Employer:

...It is our wish for you all that time will ease the terrible pain you have suffered and the knowledge that Lorie left so many friends and fond memories in London may continue to comfort you...Ray Cecil

~~~~~~~~~~~~~~~~~~~~~~

Letter from a student friend from Turkey:

...First, I don't believe. I imagine her smiles, many things...I went with her group some churches, mosques. We were gone museums, shopping to Grand Bazaar. She was bought from there some silver jewellery...She gave me rosette (which contain your country of flag). Now, she is for atheists nothing, for believers angel on the blue sky but who loves her, she is like the part of their body. But it been loosen. I wish who loves her to have patience...I will always remember Lorie with all my love.

Ali Riza Gunesdogan

~~~~~~~~~~~~~~~~~~~~~~

Letter from a friend from Greece:

Dear Mr. and Mrs Lee-Knight,

I received your letter today and I want to express my deepest sympathy for the loss of your daughter, Lorie. I telephoned you some days after I heard of her death, but there was no answer. I still can't believe that Lorie has died, and I think of her often. We became very good friends during the time she stayed in Athens, and I know what a nice person she was. I have photographs of her, and I will send them to you as soon as possible. I also enclose my address and telephone number if you want something from me. If you ever come to Greece I would like to meet you.

In deepest sympathy,
Yours sincerely, Dimitris Karaboulas

[Dimitris is the young man who worked in an Athens post office and who came to Lorie's rescue when another employee was being difficult at the time she wanted to pick up the special camera we had bought for her birthday.]

~~~~~~~~~~~~~~~~~~~~~~

Friendship Hotel
Beijing, China
July 25, 1988

… You will never know how sorry I am over your daughter's death; just as I will never know how deeply you were affected by the loss. She was a wonderful young woman. Bright, creative and talented…It was a nightmare which I'm sure we all expected would end; that somehow time would shift backwards…I believe that your daughter's life, although short, was a very full one; fuller in many ways than the lives of people who live decades longer than most. Lorie saw more, experienced more than many people ever will.... I do want you both to know that Lorie loved you very much. We did not tell you those things when we met in London just to comfort you. But because they were things she had told us. And she must have felt pretty strongly about them, or she would never have mentioned them. I hope very much that the day will come when you are both able to look back on the wonderful memories you have of Lorie with love and happiness; without pain.

~~~~~~~~~~~~~~~~~~~~~~~

From Lorie's co-worker and friend:

To Lorie's family–September 21, 1986

I sincerely hope that since we met in London some of your grief may have eased. Although those of us who called ourselves Lorie's friends can only guess at how this has affected you, I would like to say that none of us here at UBC has been unaffected.

As you no doubt are aware a memorial service was held at UBCon registration day, 5th of September, at Cecil Green Park, overlooking the water and the mountains. The service was quite brief, and wonderfully unique. Some of Lorie's favourite music (at least in London) was played along with a selection of slides of her in and around the school and in Greece. From what I knew of Lorie it was ideally suited.

When we spoke in our London office you asked me to tell you what I could about Lorie and her time in England. I am sorry there was not more opportunity to do this in person, but perhaps a letter is a more suitable way of doing this, being somewhat more permanent. I have been meaning to sit down and write this for some time, but until now have been unable to bring myself around to doing it. I have kicked myself for not taking photographs of her while in London, but I only hope that this letter may in some small way return to you what has been so tragically taken, that is a small fragment of her life, as I knew it.

I first met Lorie some two years ago, soon after she came to UBC. We shared no classes and were seated in very different parts of the studio so had little contact. I always knew who she was and spoke to her occasionally; she was just the sort of person who everybody knew and never forgot. Our first real conversation occurred during the Christmas party...We spoke a little about her growing up on the Prairies, and she was quite impressed that I remembered driving through Swift Current and actually stopped for more than just a fill-up of petrol.

Since the Christmas in 1984 I did not really speak to her until she arrived in London. One of the partners said he was interviewing a Canadian girl by the name of Laurie Wright. The next morning as I was charging through the doors into the 3rd floor studio out walked Lorie; somehow I just knew the new girl was to be Lorie. I almost did not recognize her at first; I do not remember quite why, but she was wearing her hair quite differently to how I remembered. I was thrilled to have a fellow classmate from home working with me, and she seemed as excited as I was about me showing her all the little mundane things like how to control your temper while dealing with a British bank, where to eat, where to buy a tube pass, etc.

Over the next few weeks we had lunch together almost every day in a little sandwich shop around the corner called Paninos. Lorie was blown away by the term 'Granary bap' for a large granola style bun. She soon became addicted to their tuna and avocado. I remember it was very important to her to pay her share of the tab (we alternated paying for lunch). I think this was because of all of the money problems she had encountered while travelling. I soon had other obligations and working hours so, unfortunately, our lunches together became less frequent.

I was totally astounded by how taken Lorie had been with her time on the Riviera and in Greece. With her it was not bragging, as it would have been with some others; she was just riding on an incredible high. We went out to a gorgeous Victorian pub on Charring Cross Road one night where we met up with G. I think this was about three or four weeks after she had arrived in London... I enjoyed G. and left with a good feeling about the two of them.

Towards the end of June the firm held a barbeque at the Portsmouth office. It was on a Saturday, so we decided to rent a car and do some sightseeing together that weekend. It took forever to get out of London but Lorie's sense of direction (without a map!) proved even better than mine, and we saw all sorts of wonderful areas. We managed to detour near a few housing estates the borough councils had erected which are now incredible slums. These fascinated Lorie, and she decided to investigate these for her thesis topic.

That Friday we finally found the motorway and headed for Canterbury. Along the way we stopped several times to try to phone her friend in Greece who had her portfolio, all to no avail. In Canterbury we found a terrific Tudor house/shop which had shifted so much the front door was on a 30 degree tilt. This was Lorie's first encounter with English skewed Buildings, and we must have spent half an hour photographing the crazy place. The cathedral was also quite disjointed, and the oddities of the structure combined with the voices of practising boys' choir provided us with a very memorable visit. My driving took us through a few 'pedestrian only' precincts, but Lorie never complained. In fact, she refused to drive as she was scared of her own driving!

It was becoming dark when we left but we decided to stick to the back roads and avoid the Motorways. Lorie had many wonderful qualities, but reading a map was just not one of them. However, we saw more fun and fascinating little hamlets and places that it became just a matter of heading in a general direction and seeing where we landed. We had a list of definite places to see, all examples of must-see architecture, most of which were hilariously boring. Our esteem for our employers took a major drop!

We travelled along the southeast coast until it became dark. In Eastbourne Lorie searched out a pay phone to call Greece while I located the bed and breakfast area. She was great at rolling down her window and asking directions from everybody! We must have talked to every tramp on the coast in trying to get to this hotel. It was Lorie's first taste of B and B, and we had great fun trying to convince the lady in charge that we really did want a twin room or two singles. Even then she insisted on registering us as "Mr. and Mrs.", something I never let Lorie forget. Eastbourne is a typical, yet small, English coastal town. There is the beach and cliff on one side of the main road and five storey, terraced houses and hotels on the other. Ours was quite non-descript, but still charming and typically 'quaint'.

The next day we had the best 'good English breakfast' I've encountered, and Lorie never did believe my horror stories of eggs and gristle floating in a puddle of melted lard. Just out of Eastbourne is a park called Beechy Head. It is a large grassy bluff overlooking the channel. The grass slopes up to the sheer chalk cliffs which fall down over 500 feet to the water. The wind was very strong, and I was paranoid a gust would let up and Lorie would fall forward. There are the foundations from a WW2 radar installation, and you can almost hear the Lancaster planes struggling home over the cliffs. It is quite awe-inspiring, and just as we were soaking it up an RAF helicopter squadron flew past the cliffs in formation below us. It was too beautiful to even try to photograph. Just after that Lorie burst out laughing, and I turned to see her pointing at a simple wooden bench. The English, in all of their sensible and civilized acts, had carefully placed a bench all alone in the middle of the grassy field.

No paths, bushes, or rocks; it was a park and so it needed a bench to go with the mowed grass, even though the adjacent field was wild and had flocks of grazing sheep. We had a hurried drive through Brighton and westward along the coast to Portsmouth. We finally found the office and had quite a chat with the other members of our firm. Lorie was, as usual, one of the star attractions, being a 'bloody foreigner' and also being Lorie. We begged off the game of rounders (softball) on the beach and got a tour of a Roman ruin about twenty miles away. This fascinated us both, but Lorie must have taken a dozen photographs of the tiled floors and ruined walls spread out beneath our wooden walkway inside a large modern enclosure. Coming from Canada, and in particular a more recently developed area, something as visually mundane as this ruin became a small obsession with her just because it was 2,000 years old. Her attitude refreshed my interest in the, by now, mundane buildings of London.

We finished off the afternoon by having creamed tea on a lawn in front of a hotel in an extremely English town. It made us Canucks feel that we had truly found civilization. That evening we drove the short distance to Southampton and searched for another Roman wall which we were encouraged to seek out and photograph. We made four or five trips to the taxi queue at the train station to ask directions and spent quite a time photographing this wall which was sheltering a new housing development. One part was excavated but was being left due to it being the ruined foundations of a Roman house. This untouched and unkempt pit was fenced off, and I incurred Lorie's wrath by suggesting they grass it over. She became quite outraged that I would consider destroying our 'heritage' by allowing people to use the area for walking or sitting. We never did agree, and I think she always regarded me somewhat suspiciously afterwards; in her eyes I think I had sold out to the money-grubbing developer attitude, because I saw no value in fencing off a 10' x 10' row of stones.

Our stay in another BandB, found after another two trips to the rather amused taxi queue, was less glamorous but equally comfortable as 'Mr. and Mrs. Parker'. At breakfast we were treated to a very revealing sight. A permanent resident of the hotel had two of his grandchildren staying for the week. He was in tweeds and looked all set for a stroll on the moors while these two teen-boppers were done up in punk hair styles and were acting totally oblivious of him. Apparently they had been with him for a week, and we could feel them counting the seconds. We had a huge list of places to go and see and managed through luck, to find many of them on our way. Our intended destination was Bath, and even though we only spent two or three hours there I feel somewhat relieved, if that is the suitable term, that I was able to at least contribute to Lorie seeing that wonderful city which everybody should see at least once, especially architects. The Georgian terraces and rebuilt Roman baths are truly breathtaking and we managed to sneak in an open back door to get a grand tour for free. We were also offered a rare treat as the Royal Circus and Crescent, the architectural students from Bath U., had placed some relics of statues and rather humorous artifacts on the grass.

To digress, we drove through the so-very-green English countryside along winding roads as fast as we dared. The radio station we managed to pick up near Winchester played many golden oldies, and we had great fun singing along and discussing what each one reminded us of. Very fittingly 'Winchester Cathedral' was one as was another which we hadn't heard in about five years, 'I've never been to me'. We were enjoying getting caught up on the sentimentality of it all until the last few lines when the singer spoke about how being a woman was 'holding that new baby in your arms' and 'going home to your husband'—that's the essence anyway. That, I'm afraid, made us both resolve to not listen to that song for another five years.

Winchester is a lovely city where my boss, Michael Highton, lived and commuted from every day. So, naturally, we had to visit. The cathedral was truly marvellous but was filled with a tour-bus load of (East) Indians who were shouting and crying out. This being a Sunday it grated on even my agnostic feelings (I got the impression that Lorie felt the same way). We walked around the grounds and once again lost ourselves in the maze of the streets and found some wonderful things to photograph. The next stop was Stonehenge which is adjacent to a site of a project in the office. Even more relevant for us, however, it was the weekend of the summer solstice, and a large band of 'hippies' had again tried to hold a rock concert at the monument. The police broke them away and broke up their caravan. It was all so reminiscent of the 1960's, and we were astounded at how they were treated and referred to by the media. There was a bit of excitement when we arrived as the authorities had just re-opened the grounds to all but several groups and individuals who they claimed were 'hippies'. I was all ready to photograph the injustices about to be brought to bear on these (by now) harmless people, but Lorie was ready to go in there fighting.

Stonehenge was a real treat, especially for Lorie, and so we decided to visit Banbridge, a town situated right in something similar to Stonehenge. We walked all through the area looking at the large stones erected in concentric circles before deciding it was really crazy to waste money photographing rocks and went and had more creamed tea. Somehow that made even the cold drizzle seem civilized.

The drive to Bath is truly gorgeous, and that is one thing on the trip which impressed me as much as it did Lorie. After exploring as much as we could on a Sunday we set out in search of a folly (a ruin built as a ruin in a place where somebody thought there should be a ruin to look at. 'Pure folly!' said we), and we saw a pub called 'The George' in Norton St. Philip. It is another of the several 'oldest pubs in England', but we decided it should be, as it was truly marvellous. Much like an old hunting lodge, there were high timbered ceilings and a large collection of copper and brass.

The drive back to London was quite long and tiring, but we managed to keep up the conversation between fading radio stations and the two burning cars we saw along the way (faulty wiring, we guessed). My most memorable recollections of that trip is our talks. We must have covered every topic from school to gossip to religion to being a parent (in the future) to architecture to family. I was quite impressed by the strength of Lorie's convictions and also in how they were quite innovative. I tend to be quite conservative in many ways and most 'liberal' ideas don't tend to impress me. I did not agree with a lot of what she had to say, but found I could not write them off as just repetitions of what she had heard. In a way few others I've met could, that lady could think!

Lorie seemed particularly fascinated with ways of bringing up children and how to balance that with both parents having a career. She mentioned how her parents had managed it, and she had no problems with or as a result of it. I felt that she was a person who was ready for the future.

David Lockwood had asked the two of us to present our portfolios to the firm during a lunch hour seminar, on the 4th of July! We convinced him that it might be more appropriate to show some completed Canadian projects on the 1st of July. Lorie and I spent much time working together, and she was invaluable in locating slides and convincing people to lend her things when others had always failed. When returning to the Royal Institute of British Architects' Library to try another vain attempt to borrow two badly needed books to photograph I asked her what she'd do if they refused. 'I'll cry', said she, and told me how she'd become upset in a Greek library and caused such a scene that they gave her what she wanted. That wasn't her intention there, but we were so desperate that she almost did it at the RIBA. As it tuned out we 'snuck' a camera in and illicitly photographed what is perfectly permissible in most other libraries in the world.

We had a bit of a rough time assembling the slides and having a tug-of-war over who would discuss what. We became quite tense with each other, both of us being quite head-strong, but the show was a success (even though we didn't get Lorie's coveted Prairie Oysters to inflict upon our innocent British workmates), and we soon became as friendly as ever. Unfortunately, I was moved to the 5th floor soon after so saw very little of Lorie during July and August. She always popped in to say 'Hi' when upstairs, but until the last week she was at work we rarely had a chance to get together. She temporarily moved upstairs and sat at a board in front of me on that Tuesday. We talked quite extensively about her plans and intentions for her Directed Studies and how she might go about it. I was very excited for her as I knew she would enjoy spending the time in the libraries in London and writing up her topic on social housing. In front of me she always called it socialist housing, although I never could quite figure it out, because she wasn't in favour of what they had done nor was she particularly right-wing.

The last time I saw Lorie was when she came up to the 5th floor to speak to another chap about some drawings. Apparently their drawings were not jiving, and he couldn't figure out why she kept drawing things so large. To Lorie's embarrassment she had been taking written dimensions as being in centimetres instead of the architecturally universal millimetres. I still feel a little badly about teasing her although she took it very well. We spoke of possibly meeting for lunch when we came in to collect our cheques the next day, our day off, and the last I saw of Lorie was how I most often saw her when I left the office, that is working at her board on the 3rd floor with her back to the window/door.

Ray Cecil spoke to me of the daughter he had lost, and that while sudden deaths of any nature are always a terrific shock, he was glad that your (and our) memories of Lorie were of a lovely, healthy, and vibrant lady who always brought cheer with her. I truly hope that in time this is the only type of memory you have, and also that this letter might be of at least some small value to you. If there is anything at all that I can do, please do not hesitate to ask.

With kindest regards, Rob P.

****

When Lorie's UBC classmates arranged a memorial service to be held at the Architectural School there, I was too shaken and ill after our London trip and the Swift Current service to travel to another one. Lorie's dad really wanted to attend, but he knew he needed to stay with me. The UBC students compiled an album with photos of Lorie and her class mates at work and at play. They sent it along as their gift to us. We were very moved to have visual evidence of the many people whose lives Lorie touched.

****

Urgent questions swirled unmercifully through our heads. Incredulous, we asked them of one another. What of young women who daily put their lives at risk by the very way they chose to live? How is it that they survive the dark alleys, alcohol, drugs and by keeping company with high risk lifestyle people? How can this tragedy have befallen our lovely Lorie who loved life with an exuberance few could match, our fun-loving girl, our daughter who worked and studied so hard, always striving to reach her lofty goals? Lorie, gifted artist and architect, friend of artists, architects and other professionals, as well as friend of the marginalized. Lorie, filled with appreciation for live theatre and for art of every kind…She had such plans, wanting, through her work, to create beauty and a better world. Where are all those aspirations, those dreams now? What of those others who have no such desires, no compunction to better themselves nor to help others?

Lorie should have been allowed to enjoy her adventure in London, to travel to relatives in Holland, to come home, to finish her degree at UBC, to have a promising career, marry, and have children. Lorie should have been allowed… Should have…Should have…

PART FIVE

MEMORIES

I'll lend you for a little while, a child of mine, he said, for you to love the while she lives and mourn for when she's dead. It may be six or seven years, or twenty-two or three, but will you, until I call her back take care of her for me. She will bring you charms to gladden you, and should her stay be brief, you will have lovely memories, as solace to your grief.

I cannot promise she will stay, since all from earth return, but there are lessons taught down there, I want this child to learn. I've looked this wide world over for friends and family true, and from the throngs that cross life's lane I have selected you. Now will you give her all your love, nor think your labour vain, nor hate me when I call her back again. I fancied that I heard you say, "Dear Lord, thy will be done", for all the joy thy child shall bring, the risk of grief we run. We'll shelter her with tenderness, we'll love her while we may, and for the happiness we've known, forever grateful stay. But, should the angels call for her, much sooner than we planned, we will brave the bitter grief that comes, and try to understand. Author unknown

August 8, 1987

Dear Lorie,

The calendar tells us it is a whole year since you left us. To us it seems like only last week, often it is like yesterday. The pain of your leaving is too much for us. Pain is an inadequate word, but our language has no one word that can express how we feel, your dad and I. We have been watching the calendar move steadily toward August, not wanting to think about that month, that particular day, the exact moment when we stopped being who we have been. Nothing in life prepared us for this foreign existence we suddenly had imposed upon us. Again, our language fails us when we attempt to explain where we are. It's another plane, we're here certainly and seem to be functioning, if sorrowfully, but part of us has moved into another dimension. It is a place where humans cannot go under normal circumstances. I do not understand it, I just know it is part of me and I am part of it, and I sense it always will be. I know this change has taken place because you were wrenched away from us, the parents that loved you so deeply that we really were a part of one another, and that even in dying, especially in dying, you took part of us with you. You know how I have always needed things to make sense. Well, this is how I understand what had happened to us.

This date will always be especially difficult for us, there is no hiding from it. We have wondered how we would face it. I knew for me there would be a need for quiet contemplation. I need to get in touch with my feelings and give expression to them. Your dad needs to be active in order to cope with his thoughts and the pain they give him. I've come to the cottage for a couple of days of quiet reflection. It is so peaceful here. There is a gentle breeze sighing through the woods and the sun is warm. The water is the same clean clear blue it always is, the beach stretches white and uncluttered. Today I am looking at my memory pictures of you here at the lake. How you loved to ski this lake, how strong and vital and real you were. I can see the goldenness of you emblazoned on the water's blue depth. White gulls dart off as you cut through their midst, as you carve your image on my memory. Your laughter echoes back to me through the woods as you glide gently to shore. I still see you as you were, always in motion: now jogging along the beach, then tramping along a game trail, now swimming your strong strokes, perhaps sketching quietly, then painting furiously as if there were no tomorrow. You and Todd skied along the woods one Christmas we spent here. We have a picture of you just in from the cold sitting by the fire, cheeks flushed, your eyes so bright and alive, snowflakes on your eyelashes and brow. You were nineteen. That was the Christmas we four tramped through deep snow in the woods to find just the right tree. We decided on a straight little pine that we all decorated back at the cottage.

The cottage—what a lot of planning and work we all put into it. I clearly see a day much like today, how huge and blue the sky was with the sun dappling through the woods surrounding us. We were building the floor over the cement foundation. While on your knees you pounded nails just like your dad and me. You were sixteen then.

Then there was the time that you and Todd drove all night after work to get here for a couple of days off from summer jobs. Todd had brought his big bottle of pennies just in case he ran out of gas money. You were both so tired, but you were coming to the lake—to our cottage—to us. I can see your weary happiness as we reached for one another on the driveway. We felt complete once more—we might not have recognized the feeling for what it was at the time, but now I know what it was. We thought you would sleep, wanted you to, but you were both so anxious to be out on the lake that we did not hesitate. There we were, the four of us in the boat, you and Todd fishing—you both caught fish—your dad just handling the boat, both of us just enjoying having you with us. I see you now, as then, happily and contentedly weary and limp, clasping your rods, dozing off, waking, the sun always shining on you, on your goldenness against the blue of water and sky. A precious memory of you that we thought would be repeated often over the years.

When you were sixteen, you and your girlfriend were here staying for a week. You were both so excited about being here. The first night you stayed out quite late. We were upset wondering what could have happened and were about to go looking when the two of you came strolling down the road quite unconcerned about, and unaware of, the time. You had been sitting around a campfire on the beach with friends just enjoying being here, relaxed and happy. We were short with you both and sent you to bed. I wish we could take back the anger and fear we had felt.

We felt fear for you more than once in your life, a few of those times here at the lake. Again, you were with friends, there was a minor boat mishap, and your head had been banged. We were concerned about the extent of your injury and urged you to see the physician, but you resisted as you felt a little foolish. Finally, you went and checked out okay. I did not relax until the lump receded, and your symptoms improved.

On another occasion you were thirteen plus, and Todd was sixteen. The two of you asked permission to take two friends for "a little boat ride." It was evening, and the sun was still bright so we gave permission. An unexpected fog rolled in as the sun was setting, and when we went to the beach to check on you, we were shocked there was no boat in sight. We paced the shoreline, waiting and watching; surely you would appear at any moment. Your dad commandeered a boat and driver from the lodge, and off they went searching. The men came upon you as you nonchalantly boated homeward. You had gone to the big island where the priests have a retreat. They met you all at their dock and invited you in for cake and hot chocolate. You had never been on the priests' island, and there was an opportunity to do something different. You were having an adventure, and it was still light out. How worried we had been; how we tend to worry when it is not necessary. It seems when we are not concerned that real danger and tragedy befalls us.

When we had built our large family cottage we had done it with an eye to the future, to house three generations for years to come. You and your mate, Todd and his, along with your children and theirs were to be a part of this cottage along with us. We would all come and go, congregate, have reunions. There would be barbeques on the deck that was to be built, fishing and fish fries, berry picking, wiener roasts on the outside pit and corn popping in the fireplace. There would be long, lazy days filled with activity and laughter, talking and lounging. I would read books, and you would draw and paint. All of you young people would water ski, and I would read stories to the grandchildren and tuck them into bed with promises for more sandcastle building and picnics on the beach. Your dad would take them on expeditions through the park, let them "help" as he puttered and tinkered with the boat or about the yard. The men would all help with some building project, and then they would go fishing. You would all have to return to your homes and jobs, but your dad and I would be retired and able to stay on longer. We would enjoy the quiet and the memories of us all being together knowing we would repeat these happy times over and over, knowing you would all be coming back to us.

At such times I often found myself reminiscing. I remember when we had first arrived in this area, long before we built the cottage and dreamed these dreams. In 1963 the RCMP had transferred us to the Village of Goodsoil in Northwest Saskatchewan, and Lac des Isles was just ten minutes down the road. You were only sixteen months when we brought you and your big brother here. I was in awe of the unspoiled wildness and grandeur of the dense tall forest and the expansive, picturesque lake and beaches. My fondest memories of that time are the drives that your dad took us on. Chris, then four, usually sat in the back seat with Kip, our German shepherd. You would sit on my lap or between your dad and me. You would invariably fall asleep on the drive home, stretched across my lap. I dressed you in pink quite a bit at that time, and your cheeks would be pink with sunshine and excited play. I see your pink suit and socks with white shoes. Your curly, strawberry blond hair was your crowning glory even then. You were our golden rose. I can feel your small body warmly nestled into mine, see dimples on your chubby hands, feel your warm, even breathing, see your composed sleeping-beauty face. Our dear baby girl dreaming. My cherished memories.

But my first memory of you at this lake was just a few days after we had moved to the village in the summer of 1963. Your dad had taken us on a preliminary drive of the area. A few days later I decided to take you and Chris for an outing to the lake, enchanted as I had been with my first glimpse. I parked along the beach, and the three of us took off our shoes so we could paddle in the water. I remember you were wearing a sun suit and sun bonnet to match in a blue and yellow flower design. Hand in hand we walked into the cool, clear water, excited by the beautiful new scenery around us. There were few cottages then, and not a vehicle or another person in sight. It seemed as if we three were alone in the wilderness which this lake pretty much was back then. Chris got wet, and I turned to support his tummy while he flailed his slim arms and legs. Sounds of the churning water created echoes in the stillness. You were just behind me and closer to shore, the water barely to my knees. When I turned back in perhaps twenty to thirty seconds, not more, I discovered you had passed us unnoticed since I was bent over Chris as he struggled and splashed with clenched eyes trying to keep his face out of the water.

There you were stretched out motionless, your full baby length floating with your face down in the water. Your blue floral bonnet and suit ballooned out in unison as they gently bounced with the ripples of the lake. I lunged toward you; perhaps only five or six feet separated us, but the water held my legs from moving at the speed my brain was telling them. When I reached you I grabbed a handful of blue suit and hoisted you up and out of the water. You gave a small sputter, took a deep breath and struggled to be freed. As droplets of water trickled down your face you did not seem upset, but pleasantly surprised. And that was your infamous start to your lifelong love of water sports and watercrafts. But the icy fear that had clutched my heart the moment I saw you floating inert was intense and did not quickly pass. I believe you were both confused by the intensity of my reaction as I dragged you both from the water, wrapped you in towels and hurried you into the car. You must have seen the concern on my face as I drove home. I remember thinking if anything serious had happened, there would have been no one nearby, no one to call to for help. We were alone. At some point in the scramble of bodies and towels I had tossed your drenched bonnet on top of the car, but in my hurry

I had forgotten it there. We never did see your blue bonnet again.

On the drive home I swore to myself that you and your brother would have swimming lessons and lots of opportunity to practise. In the years that followed I kept that promise; you both became excellent swimmers, life guards and swim instructors.

But why had I reacted so extremely all those years ago? Even I knew it was over reaction. But I seemed unable to stop myself. Did some part of me know that eventually your life would end in water? Mirroring your first lake experience, there would be no one to come to your aid. I only pray that you did not suffer for long and that you trusted God to the end, trusted like a child trusts.

Love Always, Mom

~~~~~~~~~~~~~~~~~~~~~~~~

Hello Lorie—Today I finally opened your backpack with its tattered maple leaf flags you so proudly displayed while travelling in Europe. I have found your meagre wardrobe that you had recently acquired—mostly cheap, but stylish and color coordinated—pathetic in the small number of pieces because you had just started to buy a few needs with your own, well-earned money. Soon you would have paid off the small debt you had incurred and would have been able to shop with greater joy and less thriftiness for the first time in your life. What fun to shop and what pride you would have felt knowing it was your very own money you were using. The delphinium-blue silk blouse with padded shoulders had been very recently purchased as the price tag was still attached. Its good quality was reflected in its price. What a pleasure it must have been for you to select it, try it on and then have it bagged. I can see the pleasure on your face as you walked down the busy London street with your few parcels. Did you imagine how you would look in the blouse, what accessories would go with it, what G. would say when he saw you in it? I can see you wearing it even now, every head turning at seeing your gorgeous golden and vibrant hair just touching the shoulders of the sleek, blue fabric...

Love, Always, Mom

****

Thursday, November 17, 1988 was a special sort of day. A few days before, I had been feeling unwell with a bad cold. Jack had just returned home unexpectedly after having been up north for several days working on our cottage. I was especially relieved to see him so he could accompany me to Morse, a small town near Swift Current, to attend the closing reception for Lorie's exhibition there. I showed him the large article on *The Compassionate Friends* (parents who have lost children) that had appeared in the Swift Current newspaper. Their reporter had come to our home to interview another mother and me about this new chapter we had recently formed.

The next day, while Jack was at work, Lorie's art pieces were returned from Morse. It was emotionally difficult for me as I helped carry the several framed works downstairs for temporary storage. Soon after, the phone rang; it was a woman to tell me about her grandson who had won the Lorie Lee-Knight Scholarship that year. He was very happy to be studying at the Emily Carr School of Art in Vancouver, and he had earlier written to thank us for the scholarship.

Then I received a call from a mother who said she had seen the *TCF* newspaper article and told me she had lost a child to SIDS some time ago. She had a book and information on SIDS to donate to our society's library. While we spoke another call came in. This second mother told me she had seen the article and that she had lost a baby to SIDS. She was interested in attending the next meeting and wanted more details about our chapter. That day's mail brought a donation to help set up the *TCF* chapter. When Jack returned home he told me of the generous amount the funeral home had donated. I showed him the acceptance note that had arrived that day from the Western People magazine for a poem I had written entitled *You Live*. In pain and through tears I had written it the day I had escaped to the cottage on the first anniversary of Lorie's death. All these incidents occurring on the same day left me reeling. God must have been very close to us that day, and I believe Lorie was too. I took that day's occurrences as more assurance that Lorie was safe with her Lord.

****

You Live

Yesterday
I could still cast back
still tell my heart
call it to the open sky—
a year ago today
you lived
But today is
one year later
I raise my headache
from bed of tears
sip burning coffee
feel drawn to water's edge
breathe Lac des Isles chill
sun rises still warms me

loon speaks of mystery
your lake lies gentle misty
guarded by distant piney shore
gentle puffs of cloud
frame this picture you painted
so many times in varying light
squirrels pass my quiet pose
dart watch chatter
perform as every day
birch bark drapes its curls
fall asters nod mauve heads
tree roots spread giant hands
through plush moss
it's all the same just as you saw
as you breathed it in recorded
with brush
became a part of it and it of you
so as I breathe it in record with pen
you are part of me and I of you
this real way our spirits join
forever
this real way
you live

****

A letter from Lorie came into my thoughts as clearly as if it had been written:

Dear Mom, Dad and Todd,

I left three years ago—left you and Dad and Todd when I died. But I'm still me—I feel like I did when I was on earth—only better, more alive. There are no words that living humans can understand, there where you are, to express how wonderful I feel, how beautiful it is here. You can't know until you are here with me—I would tell you if there were words, if you could understand. But you will be with me again, and together we will explore the wonder of it. I am still with you and Dad—in your hearts all the time. You feel me there—know I will always be there. I feel your struggle to live on, so burdened with the sorrow that my leaving has given you. And I need you to know that besides being alive in your hearts, I am Alive—really Alive. And I want you to know that here I am not lonely or sad or worried or pressured or depressed or in pain. I am with my grandparents and other relatives, with friends who I knew there and new friends I have met here. We are all soul mates together.

It will not be a long time before you and Dad are here with me, and you will understand everything. It might seem you are there for a long time, but you will see it is nothing in comparison. Until then I can only be more real to you in your sleep or in the quiet of the woods and the lake. You feel me closer to you at those times? Together we watch the beauty of a deer, of trees, of the sunsets on the lake, you and dad and I. Until then I can only come very near you, Dad, as you build things with your hands. I can only touch your tired arms ever so lightly when you doze off in your chair after a day of hard work. Until then I can show you and Mom that you must not worry about me, because I am fine, better than Fine. You know I am close by when you see the clouds form into the same sideways cross that I painted and that hangs in your home.

Todd, you know I am with you when you sail over the lake on your surf sail, water skies or when speeding down a snowy hill. You need to seek the joy of that freedom on the water or on the hills that I knew sailing and skiing. When you are most alone, that is when I am with you and we sail and ski free. I walk with you, Mom, crossing a meadow, then through tall wild grass or following a game trail in the woods to photograph that special sight. Together we view the best angle to shoot from, share the pleasure in seeing the results just as we planned. We capture nature scenes together with your camera that once was mine, that you and Dad bought for my last birthday. Together we see beauty of line and shadow and texture and colour, so you can share with me the experience of my drawings and paintings. The passion I felt there for art, you share in your writing. Do you feel me urging you on?

I feel your regrets, your feelings of guilt, your pain—yours and Dad's, and I want to take that all away from you—I want you to know I understand. You wish you had loved more, tried harder and been better parents. There is no need. You gave me more of yourselves than any parents I knew—you sacrificed for me—I knew that then, but it is ever so much clearer here. You encouraged me, even at times when no one else had any faith in me or my plans. You were frightened for me when I showed no sign of being cautious. You protected me as much as I would let you. You loved me when I would not listen—you knew I had to follow my heart—you supported me always. I wish life could have been easier for us all then, wish I could make it more bearable for you now. I love you all so much. I was so proud of you then and prouder of you now. I want you all to enjoy life there as much as you can–to get the most out of every experience just as you allowed me to do.

Remember, I am always with you, but will be waiting with big hugs when it is time for each of you to join me. God is in charge.

With eternal love, Lorie Gaye

~~~~~~~~~~~~~~~~~~~~~~~

Dear Lorie,

Here are some thoughts of you I want to share:

You chose many friends from minority groups; you did so in a natural and unconscious way before it became a popular choice to make. Soon after starting school you became friends with an Asian girl and a Métis girl. In another school you became fast friends with a lovely girl of Chinese ancestry, and you remained friends for the rest of your life. During your university years in Vancouver you lived with a Japanese-Canadian lady and became close friends with her and her family. A black girl lived in the same house and you befriended her as well as a neighbour who was by choice a single mother. You understood her decision to deliberately become pregnant even though she did not wish to marry. That lady and the Japanese roommate wrote us most sincere letters expressing their love for you and their great sorrow at your death.

I think back to the time I was a little surprised when you told me that you had become friends with two homosexual hair stylists and what good people you found them to be. You bartered one of your beautiful, oil pastoral scenes for some hair styling appointments. The stylists attended your art exhibition at the university where you introduced them to me. They were pleasant to chat with, and I was proud of you for taking the opportunity to discover their humanity. After talking with them

I realized I had removed another barrier I had unconsciously placed between myself and much of the world around me. And I thank you for this special gift.

Much love, Mom

****

From Mom With Love by Ruth Lee-Knight was first published in Saskatchewan Woman Magazine, October/ November 1992 issue. Six years after losing our daughter we were still struggling with many unresolved feelings. It is important to me to draw attention to the insensitivity exhibited by some people following a death due to a sexual attack. I want to set the record straight in showing that women are not always (perhaps seldom) responsible for such attacks. I hope people will think twice before making insensitive and hurtful comments thereby sparing the survivors additional pain.

Dear Lorie,

You know how difficult it is for your dad and I since you were taken from us. Life without you continues to be a daily struggle for us. The cruel way in which you died is far more than we can come to terms with. You and many other beautiful, talented and worthy young women have had your lives snuffed out by the senseless acts of sex offenders.

There have been thoughtless remarks and questions to which we and other parents have been exposed. "Was he a friend of hers?" is one that drives us mad, and "How did he get in?" is another. "Why didn't she fight?" leaves us livid. It's extremely hard for us to remain civil when faced with such insensitivity. We do our best to relate how you, as an educated young professional, moved in a circle of the educated and sophisticated in London, England. We explain how you were attacked in your home by a criminal who had recently been released from jail where he had been serving time for other sexual offences. His other victims continued to live. You were alone and he gained access to the building, not a difficult thing for a chronic criminal.

I could tell them how your own boyfriend had encouraged you to move in with him, but that you had declined. You wrote us about that and said, "I'd rather stay in my own little place for now."

We were so proud of your decision and of your desire for independence. Since that dreadful day in 1986 we have often wished your decision had been otherwise. But living with someone would not have guaranteed your safety either. You could still have been caught alone and defenceless one hour of another day.

And didn't they think you fought and struggled against the perpetrator of that heinous crime with every breath you had? Fought until he squeezed the very breath out of you just because you fought? Scotland Yard told us that an awful struggle had taken place, but how would it be otherwise? You fought like others before you and since. You fought for your very life, and how can anyone even imagine what that must be like?

Even though you lost the terrible struggle, and your dad and I have felt so helpless and ineffectual ever since, there are those who, recognizing the evil and injustice of such a crime, are carrying on your struggle. They understand that not every female who is sexually assaulted, whether she lives or dies as a result, is "living on the street," lacks virtues, keeps unsavoury company, practices unsafe habits or haunts shadowy districts. There are more groups demanding that our society change to one where each individual who happens to be born female does not automatically run the risk of being sexually assaulted some time in her life, run the risk of being strangled to death because she fights for her life.

Attitudes are difficult to change and that must happen before females can begin to feel safe in the community, at their work place, school or even in the sanctity of their homes. I believe these groups can make a difference if they keep up their profile and continue to demand change.

When change comes it will be too late for you and your dad and me. You will never again phone excitedly from Europe to tell us of your travels there; you can't continue to explore the history and charm of England; you will never transform another canvass into a bold and beautiful work of art; it is too late for the world to benefit from new architectural structures you would have contributed. We can never again meet you at the airport or bus depot and feel your warm, vital body folded in our embrace. I can never again share those late night conversations about the mystery of life and the world. Your dad will never feel your fingers ruffle his hair "hello" or feel your soft lips brush his cheek. He will never know the pride of leading you down the aisle to your waiting groom. I can never experience the special closeness that a mother has with her daughter surrounding the birth of a child nor share the joy with your dad of being grandparents to any child you may have had.

Others will benefit from a change in society's attitude. Perhaps your very life and the publicity surrounding its cruel loss created part of the driving force that serves to seek and establish change. When you were born we had such hopes and dreams for you, and at the time of your death you were just starting to feel your wings. None of us suspected that your life might serve a bigger purpose. We can only pray that it was not in vain.

All my love,
Mom

"Life is short, Art is forever"
by Seneca

Her life was short, but packed with living.
taken from us cruelly she left priceless gifts.
bright pulsing light hidden—
still, her flame burns in all who loved her.
we see her no more, but she is always with us.

****

Shadows

sun paints water different hues each night
woods close in snug around loons call
flames dance patterns on dear faces
coffee cups steam there's talk, laughter

i see you in shadows there, hear your voice echo
imagine the lake's reflection in your eyes
feel you capture the moment's beauty
commit it to canvass where it lives

before sleep I know the forest comes alive
owls hoot, bears pass in silence
pines whisper as darkness descends
but in the quiet i feel you near

i thank God for sharing you
before you returned to Him and nature
from where you reach out to me in love
and where you help paint the skies

do you travel with deer in the night?
move in the pines, whisper with them
telling me you are always close?
do you try to comfort me as tears return?

you and i share every rainbow, every song
we walk together along wooded trails
are enchanted by perfumed roses
feel heightened awareness of nature's gifts

when others think i am alone
we will listen to early morning ravens call
watch the sun crest pine forests
mist lift from meadows

when i feel old and sad, when there is pain
i will search for you
in the flowers of my mind where trees sway
and where you wait until my own sun sets

****

.... how I carried you on eagles' wings and brought
you to myself". I recall how, as a teenager, Lorie
asked me about the significance of the eagle in
churches. None of us knew back then how it would
apply to her life and death. How it applies to all
believers.

Exodus 19: 3 - 4

POST SCRIPT

Surviving

How did my husband and I survive the pain brought by the tragedy in our lives?

After sharing the first draft of the manuscript with friends it came to my attention that people who have experienced destructive pain following a loss, or those whose family member or friend was in that situation, or, indeed, people who wonder how they, themselves, could possibly survive and/or cope—all these people and more would want to know how my husband and I survived, what kept us going, how we made a life for ourselves, a life with direction and purpose, with some measure of quality. To answer this question I must, once again, delve deep into my heart and soul to find the truths that lodge there. What I found was love.

It was love for our daughter and for one another that has Jack and I supporting each other, something like two cards in a house of cards. The house kept collapsing around us, but we just knew we had to continue to pull each other up repeatedly. We persevered. We had another child to live for; our love for our son helped us survive; we had to be there for him as he struggled with the realization that he was now an only child. Our faith, though at times wavering, did grow and seemed always to uphold us.

It is not as if we are completely healed nor do we ever expect to be. There are delightful memories of our daughter that bring a wistful smile to our faces. Many sights and sounds often bring renewed pain. As the pain washes through us we sometimes allow it to open dark thoughts with all the questions of why, why Lorie, why us. But, more often, we push the pain and lost hopes aside as we concentrate on the present. We know our girl would want us to live life to the fullest, to get the most out of every opportunity, every experience, just as she did. So, once again, love reigns—love for our lost child. We will carry on living for her because we can—and because she cannot.

I have always believed that most things happen for a reason. Cause and effect starts up a huge domino movement of incidents and experiences in life that are traced back to a particular event. I believe other things do not happen as if they were supposed to, but none the less, those incidents also set off their own chain reactions. It seems to me these latter events result in rebounding and profound reactions serving to create deep and meaningful changes in the lives of many people. My own habit of occasional journaling was never intended for anything more. But following the destruction of my old self—who I had been—what survived was much like the results of a forest fire. Wrapped deep within small spruce cones scattered about in the blackened ruins there are tiny cells of life.

New life that begins to emerge from the cones eventually creates a fresh, healthier and more beautiful environment than the destroyed one. I feel at one with that forest. During the early days of my grieving I found myself pouring strong emotions onto paper for no purpose other than to pull them out of myself where I could examine them and understand them for what they were. Looking back I know I was searching for purpose in my life and ways to continue living. When I found a writing course being offered in Swift Current, it represented a new beginning for me. I discovered I enjoyed the writing process, and that humble start of pleasure developed into love. Early on, our instructor emphasized "write what you know", those words becoming a mantra. As I gave myself permission to write what I knew, the feelings I uncovered from places deep within me crowded to be recognized and lifted to the surface where they gained expression.

Sharing with other people some of these deeply imbedded emotions came with a sense of clarity and lightness. After listening to my work or reading it people would sometimes tell me personally or write to tell me how much they had been touched by what I had written. I treasure those times and those letters because reaching others in that way gives my work validation. These small beginnings gave me confidence to continue writing. I took writing classes and joined other writers groups in Saskatoon where we then lived. Several pieces of my work, both poetry and prose, appeared in literary magazines and periodicals. My work was also published in seven anthologies. I felt ready to produce my own book in 2005, and it has been very successful.

Writing has become a passion for me, giving me a method of expression that brings much satisfaction. I compare my new life to that coming from the despair of a blackened forest. This life includes an even greater love of nature, more empathy for others in pain or with dire needs, greater tolerance for, and inclusion of, other races, religions or life styles. I am, like my writing, a work in progress. I am always aware that there can never be an end or satisfaction with "what is," but believe life is a continuum of striving.

Writing from the heart is often heart wrenching, and creating this book is no exception. It took great determination and some strength to approach the trunk containing Lorie's papers. I sorted through drawings, notes, letters, and university assignments. There were several packages of architectural photos, personal photos of Lorie and her friends as well as hardcover diary accounts. My heart broke open, as did the dam of tears, as I faced this lost life and its wonderful potential reduced to existence in a storage trunk. It took several starts, always ending in emotional exhaustion, before I worked through all the trunk's material. Again, it was only love that drove me down those stairs and into the storage room time and again. Lorie's life story needed to be told, and I knew I was the only one who could tell it. She deserved my effort; it was the least I could do for her, and this writing has taken precedence over everything these past several months. It has become my particular passion.

Jack shares my great love of nature as seen in the many birdhouses he has built, and the great sacks of birdfeed he keeps on hand. All summer he keeps feeders supplied and they attract flocks of pretty song birds, their melodious chorus gladdening our hearts. We enjoy all species of birds from tiny hummingbirds to loons with their haunting call, and great pelicans floating by our shore. Some of Jack's pain and energy went into construction of our cottage addition and into building our summer business. He has maintained and improved these buildings over the years. He continues to pay special attention to the grounds of our cottage as he did at our business that we eventually sold.

Jack's other form of release goes into doing things for others. For two years he served as president of Saskatoon's RCMP Veterans Association and for another two years held the same position in Calgary. He worked hard for our church, St. John's Cathedral, in Saskatoon. His legacy there is a new and greatly improved kitchen in the cathedral's parish hall. Another legacy is the four-faced clock and clarion bells in the cathedral's steeple. Jack was known for his admirable fund raising abilities which he put to good use to finance these projects. While president of the Saskatoon RCMP Veterans Association he envisioned the construction of a replica RNWMP detachment in that city's Western Development Museum. He raised funds for that project by explaining his vision to a number of the city's business people. He worked alongside other volunteer veterans until the detachment was completed. The opening ceremony on June 7, 2000 was well attended with greetings from dignitaries including Lt.-Governor Linda Haverstock. The gala dinner that evening was attended by a capacity crowd, and head table guests included RCMP Commissioner Philip Murray. Kerry Kutz, songstress and a former member of the RCMP Band, sang our national anthem and later supplied a delightful musical interlude. The RNWMP detachment, complete with a life-sized horse at the detachment hitching post, attracts thousands of tourists each year. A uniformed, life-sized police mannequin sitting at his desk, speaks when a tourist presses a button located near the desk. In order to understand living and working conditions of that era, visitors view the office, cells and living quarters of the constable. Jack volunteers at Fort Calgary meeting the public and answering their questions about the Force's history. He also serves on the fort's board of governors.

Jack's own pain and disability as result of an on duty motor vehicle accident has given him added empathy and understanding of the needs of others. Whenever a member of the association is ill or otherwise needy Jack readily assists in appropriate ways. He helps others cope with the search for specific assistance and with filling out medical or legal forms.

Our two grandchildren continue to be a joy for us and it has been a privilege to watch them grow and mature over the years. We have acted as their sitter, chauffer or cheering section at sports events. We celebrate Christmas, birthdays and other special times with our family. I began this postscript speaking of love. And love continues to be the driving force for us every day. That is how Jack and I have survived and how we continue on.

****

Readers may wonder if we have forgiven the man who took our daughter's life. I cannot say that we have, nor are we convinced that God expects us to. However, through our painful experience, we have learned to more easily forgive others who have wronged us in some way. We know that is the only path to acquire our own peace of mind, and if that is all we are capable of, then perhaps God will forgive us for our other weakness. We are, after all, still works in progress.

POST SCRIPT II

I looked forward to telephoning Howard and Jean Green the morning of February 9. They had just returned from a vacation the day before. We first met them when we attended St. John's Cathedral in Saskatoon, and over the years got to know them well. We spoke about my new book manuscript and they were receptive to the idea of reading it with the purpose of writing a commendation for the book's back cover.

After church the next day I took my memory stick to the print shop where they would print out a hard copy and finish it with covers and coil binding. Monday morning I felt anticipation as I went to pick up the manuscript copy, and again when I addressed the packing envelope at the post office.

Tuesday brought several email pages of matter from my publisher. I was to study it and start the work of answering questions and supplying my ideas and intentions for the book. I could see this would keep me working for several days with breaks for phone conversations with the publishing staff before doing the final work on Adobe Reader. Later that day our travel tickets arrived for our trip to Los Cabos, Mexico. I had some shopping to do for articles for the trip and had lots of decisions about a suitable wardrobe. Everything seemed to be crowding in and I was beginning to doubt the wisdom of us going away when I had so much to do. I felt frustrated and weary. That's when Rev. Ottrey phoned us. Jack answered and handed me another phone. It was the second time our friend had surprised us with a call from the Bahamas, the winter residence for him and his wife. He has the gift of knowing when people need a special word from a kind friend. I explained how I was feeling, and just as he always does, he spoke gently and with encouragement. Then he prayed with us as only Ivor does; we felt better just hearing his sincere words. I felt the very presence of the Holy Spirit and that feeling lasted for days.

****

Wednesday was February 13 and I always remember it as the date in 1962 when our daughter was due to be born. Now I was busy with household duties and was slated to attend a gathering of neighbor ladies. My back was painful that day and I did not feel up to attending, but I felt I should make an appearance. I tried to get into the spirit of the afternoon with the ladies, but I did not stay very long. There seemed to be a cloud hanging over me and I silently prayed that the Spirit would give me direction to help me out of this feeling. I applied heat on my back and before going to bed I took an analgesic tablet. I hoped that tomorrow would be a better day. I had a restless night and awoke still tired.

After breakfast on the fourteenth I phoned my publisher with some questions, then made two calls to confirm that on the coming Sunday appropriate flowers would be placed on the altar in memory of Lorie. In my mind she always will be our Valentine baby, and back in 1962 I had hoped she would be born on that day. Soon after my calls the phone rang. I answered to hear a voice with a strong accent. The man was calling from Ireland, a reporter with the Irish Sun. I immediately called Jack to pick up on a extension line and when we were both ready Fergus O'Shea apologized for disturbing us and for coming as a "blast from the past."

He wanted to let us know that George Ireland, "that evil man" had died in prison in London. He apologized again, but felt we would want to know and was concerned that we might not hear of the news otherwise. We could tell he was a kind and caring man, and we thanked him graciously. He gave us his newspaper's web site so we could view the article about our daughter's attacker to be printed the next day. We also asked for his email address so we could thank him appropriately later. We went into a bit of shock trying to digest the news, and we felt ourselves reliving the horror of the past. That was our Valentine's Day.

EXCLUSIVE:

The Sun/Irish News

Published 15 February 2013/

STEPHEN IRELAND'S SEX KILLER GRAND-UNCLE DIES IN PRISON

The body of deviant George Ireland will return in secret back home to his native Cobh today.

Pervert George, 56 died in a British prison last week where he was serving life for the brutal sex killing of Canadian student Lorie Lee-Knight in 1986.

The 24 year-old architecture student was in London for just eight weeks when Ireland strangled her in August 1986–the same month and year his grand-nephew Stephen was born.

Jobless fisherman George had fled to London after serving part of a ten-year sentence for two rapes in Ireland.

The deviant went on a spree of groping and molesting woman in subway stations before he broken into Lorie's bed sit and choked her in the bath.

Ireland's body is to arrive on board an 11:35 am fight from Heathrow to Cork Airport. It will be collected by undertakers and taken straight to the town's cemetery for burial.

A source said: "Everything is being done under a cloak of secrecy. Even close friends of the Ireland family did not know that George was dead, never mind the fact that his remains were being brought back home to Cobh. There were no announcements either in the Church or in the paper".

The source added: "The Ireland family are very well-liked and respected in Cobh. Stephen's dad Michael served in the Irish Navy and is the salt of the earth.

George was a sick man. They knew there was something wrong with him from an early age and tried to get him professional help, which was not readily available all those years ago."

Aston Villa midfielder, Stephen, has said he did not know his grand-uncle George and had no knowledge about his horrifying crimes. It is not known if he will attend his uncle's burial today.

Lorie's parents last night thanked the Irish Sun for letting them know about the killer's death in prison.

****

Jack was away attending a funeral so I was alone the afternoon of the fifteenth.

That day would have been Lorie's birthday and although I knew it was twenty-six years since we lost her, I always envision her as the young and beautiful person she was. I also knew the article about the murdering pervert would be available to me at the touch of my keypad. I kept putting it off until I felt I could summon the strength to read of her attacker's death. After doing so I felt I needed to share the message with my family and friends. I was not yet ready to speak of it so I sent out emails. Within minutes I received supportive and caring messages. Many people express the thought that with the new information Jack and I will have some needed closure. I believe it will take quite some time for Jack and I to firstly digest the news. We never expect to have full closure, but perhaps someday one of the many daggers will fall from our hearts. Nevertheless, the messages helped sustain me through the day. I kept busy with the work my publisher provided and spent a long time filling out their forms on Adobe Reader.

****

The next day a new friend, unaware of our present situation, phoned and asked how I was. I blurted out the truth and she wasted no time in breaking into a passionate prayer for Jack and me. I was grateful for her sincere help in the form of prayer. By the time Jack returned from running errands, and I had supper prepared I was feeling unnerved and very tired. We both slept somewhat better that night.

I knew that Sunday's church service would be an emotional time for us, but I also knew that the presence of the Holy Spirit would help us. As we entered the sacristy I felt the warmth of members of the congregation I had confided in and I welcomed their hugs and words of encouragement. The service was meaningful and uplifting, but by the time we joined with the congregation in sharing the Peace, I could feel tears welling up. As I tried to calm myself an announcement was made: "The flowers on the alter were given by Jack and Ruth Lee-Knight to the Glory of God and in loving memory of their daughter, Lorie." That's when the tears came in earnest. After we said the last prayer there were more hugs and kind words coming our way. I was further touched by being given one of the floral arrangements.

Back at home I looked around wondering how to proceed with my day. My glance rested on a calendar with a comforting prayer or phrase for each day of the year. The calendar had been given to me by our kind friends and cottage neighbours, Beverlie and Barry. February 17th offered the anonymous comment: "Amid the winds and fires of my day, may I pause to hear your stillness speak." With the thoughts of Valentine's Day still with me another quote stood out: "I will give them one heart, and put a new spirit within them." ~ Ezekiel 11:19

Amen

CPSIA information can be obtained at www.ICGtesting.com
Printed in the USA
LVOW05s0916061113

360122LV00002B/24/P